ORLANDO
CITY OF DREAMS

The tradition of having swans on Orlando's lakes began in 1910 at Lake Lucerne, but soon pairs of the beautiful birds were at Lake Eola, too. Neat handwriting on the back of this photo identifies the family group as "Uncle Bert, Alvin, and Sixtoe at Lake Eola," in February 1913.

THE MAKING OF AMERICA

ORLANDO
CITY OF DREAMS

JOY WALLACE DICKINSON

ARCADIA
PUBLISHING

First published 2003
Reprinted 2006

Published by Arcadia Publishing
Charleston SC, Chicago IL, Portsmouth NH, San Francisco CA

Library of Congress control number: 2003107133

For all general information contact Arcadia Publishing at:
Telephone 843-853-2070
Fax 843-853-0044
E-Mail sales@arcadiapublishing.com
For customer service and orders:
Toll-Free 1-888-313-2665

Visit us on the Internet at www.arcadiapublishing.com

CONTENTS

ACKNOWLEDGMENTS

The preparation of *Orlando: City of Dreams* has confirmed my belief that people who enjoy and support the study of history and the publication of books are among nature's noble men and women: the finest of mentors, colleagues and pals. My thanks extend far beyond the number of people it is possible to mention here.

Among colleagues past and present at *Orlando Sentinel*, I am grateful to many, including Jim Buynak, Rick Brunson, Jim Clark, Jay Davis, Nancy Pate, Manning Pynn, and especially to Mark Andrews, my predecessor in writing the "Florida Flashback" history column, and Jim Robison, my editor. Both have been exceptionally generous guides and collaborators.

Most visibly through many of the photographs that follow, this book has benefited from the assets and aid of the Orange County Regional History Center, led by Sara Van Arsdel, and the History Center's partner, the Historical Society of Central Florida, Inc. Sara and the other good folks at the History Center have buoyed my voyages into Florida history, and I thank all of you. I am especially indebted to Bob Beatty, Pat Birkhead, Tana Porter, and Cynthia Cardona Melendez, photo archivist par excellence, and to the "history warriors" of the Orlando Remembered group, especially Andy Serros and Jack Kazanzas. Thanks, too, to Leslie Sheffield of the Florida Photographic Collection in Tallahassee, one of the state's great treasures, and to Lynn Poche and James Kilby for excellent assistance with the many images gleaned for the book. Jean Yothers and Eleanor Fisher of the pioneering Bumby family were kind enough to share memories and ideas. So many seekers and supporters of Central Florida's past have offered inspiration, including Lorelei Anderson-Francis, Francina Boykin, Mary Jackson Fears, Bob Kealing, Carl Patterson, Marianne Popkins, Steve Rajtar, Rod Reeves, Henry Swanson, and the members of the West Orange Reconciliation Task Force.

So many thanks to my mother, Jean Wallace Dickinson, who early fostered my love of books and the idea that women could do anything they put their minds to. Bill, Rachel, and Elizabeth Dickinson have offered gifts of time, love, and support. Friends and wise counselors who eased the way included Anne Berry, Jennifer Greenhill-Taylor, Joseph Hayes, Nancy Kiger, and other members of the Orlando Group reading circle, and, especially, Nancy Ogren. Glenn Link, friend of my heart, offered constant support and superb advice.

I am thankful to Arcadia Publishers for reinvigorating local history in America and offering readers fresh evidence that a great photograph can speak volumes. Special thanks to Sarah Williams for signing this book and to Jim Kempert, Rob Kangas, and Barbie Langston of Arcadia for shepherding it through publication.

Of necessity, many vital names and events wait outside these pages for future efforts by me or other writers to tell their stories. That's part of the fun of history: There's always more to explore on the path to the past, waiting around the bend.

INTRODUCTION

Surely, almost everyone in America has heard of Orlando, and millions have visited. Yet this city smack in the middle of Florida may be the least known of well-known American locales. Folks of all ages from Maine to Modesto can tell you Orlando is where you go to visit Walt Disney World and the other entertainment giants that arrived in Disney's wake after 1971. It's likely many of these visitors have passed through Orlando International Airport, where the recorded voice that greets visitors speaks in the same cheery cadences heard at Disney. "Please stand clear of the doors and hold on to the handrail. Welcome to Orlando!"

It's great to be the country's vacation playground, but longtime Orlandoans periodically wince at the realization that most visitors think "Orlando" is little more than a concrete vista of tee-shirt shops huddled around the Magic Kingdom, or a behemoth convention center where they spent a hectic few days. Orlandoans revel in their role as host to America at play, but they would like people to know there is more. Their city has a history.

Orlando began its role as a city of dreams long before its theme-park era began with Walt Disney World's debut in October 1971. For well more than a century, Florida's largest inland city has lured visitors and settlers alike with the promise of a respite from everyday woes or a better life under sunny skies.

Its allure combined the familiar and the exotic, in a Shangri-la for everyday folks. Despite enclaves of wealthy residents, Central Florida never was a Palm Beach, a place for swells to winter. Middle-class Americans have always felt at home in Orlando and Orange County, Florida. At the same time, there's still enough of a tropical tang in the air for people to feel a sense of adventure, to cut loose a bit, or to seek a fresh beginning.

Some sought to make their fortune in citrus, the sweet treasure that gave the county its name. Some came driving herds of cattle to a land resembling the Old West more than the Old South. Indeed, over the years, the free-spirited promise of the frontier drew many pioneers to Orlando. In the early years, they were cowboys and Indian fighters; later, they were men and women eager to put down roots in a sunny place where dark memories of a Depression and great war might soon be forgotten.

One of them was my grandfather, William McKinley Wallace. He was a classic Floridian: a mixture of South and North who had not been born in the state but claimed it as his own. In the hopeful years after World War II, his Florida dreams had the power to transport his wife, mother, daughter and son-in-law—my parents—and me, from a small town near Pittsburgh to the land of sun and sand.

After searching the state, he and my dad had picked Orlando, in the heart of Florida—not a high-riding coastal town, but the sort of place where the houses looked like the ones back home. In Orlando, Northerners could feel at home. People from almost anywhere could.

ORLANDO

We arrived right after Labor Day in 1949. Although my mother came to love Central Florida, she remembers stepping from the cool of our Pullman train car into the full-blast heat of early September. She thought she had stepped into the gates of hell.

Not Bill Wallace. In some of my earliest memories, I am sitting on his knee in Pennsylvania while he quizzes me, "Now, where are you going to college?" "University of Florida" came the well-rehearsed reply. When the time came years later, I went to Florida State University, but it was all the same to him. It was in Florida, his final and favorite home.

"Florida was the last Eastern pioneer state," a book on the state proclaimed in 1947. My granddad's pioneering spirit came from the hills of eastern Tennessee, where in 1897, he was born in a log cabin. I saw it the summer I was 10 years old. It had one room and yellowed newsprint pages pasted on the inside walls for insulation. Somehow he made it from the log cabin to King College in Bristol, Tennessee, and then north to the land of railroads and steel mills to seek his fortune. He married Alice Swanson, a daughter of Swedish immigrants, and worked long years in sales in the steel industry, traveling cold gray roads through the Jazz Age, the Depression, and World War II. He did well in sales, could sell ice to Eskimos. No one could tell a shaggy-dog story, deliver a punch line, like him.

It's not clear when he first heard the call of Florida. Maybe it was from his boss, a millionaire who had a South Florida retreat. Maybe he read about the last Eastern pioneer state in one of the magazines he devoured. However the dream came to him, he refused to let it go. After several years of exploratory trips and campaigning to his reluctant wife, he got us all here that hot September.

He and my dad bought a grocery market on U.S. Highway 17-92 in Winter Park. They knew nothing about being grocers, but they figured people had to eat. Now they were the bosses, even if they weren't millionaires. In 1949, their new domain had sawdust floors, bushel baskets of oranges, striped awnings. The only air-conditioning came from afternoon breezes. They sold fresh orange juice and coconut milk to the tourists.

My grandfather had more than 20 good years in Orlando. I don't think it ever disappointed him. He worked shirtless in his yard in baggy shorts and sandals. He drove an aqua convertible and planted a palm tree behind his home near Lake Eola. Remarkably, it survived killer freezes and is still there, decades later. He sold trees outside the market at Christmas and bright gladioluses inside all the time. He whistled lovely melodies in the sun.

He told his stories at the market to salesmen with nicknames like "Big Tiny," and to fellow members of the Lion's Club at fish fries on cool fall evenings. Pappy Wallace, everyone called him. When he became a Lions' district governor, they gave him a patchwork Seminole jacket—genuine, made on the reservation, a symbol of true Florida spirit.

In Orlando, the city of dreams, he found a place to blossom, as had so many others like him, before and after. This is their story.

Chapter One

LA FLORIDA PRIMEVAL

If history had gone a little differently, Americans might be sitting down to a feast of seafood and salsa to celebrate Thanksgiving, instead of dining on turkey and pumpkins and other dishes we imagine to be pilgrim fare. For it was La Florida, the conquistadors' land of the flowers, that was Europe's first frontier in North America. Legends say the pursuit of gold and youth-giving waters long ago drew Spanish explorers to the land that lures so many folks today to have fun in Orlando, Florida's largest inland city. The Spanish arrived well before the English hit Massachusetts or Jamestown. By the time the pilgrims landed on Plymouth Rock in 1620, the Florida city of St. Augustine, founded in 1565, had been around for more than half a century.

On September 8, 1565, Spanish explorer Pedro Menendez de Aviles joined in the celebration of a mass in the St. Augustine area, followed by a meal when his men supped with local natives. That, historian Michael Gannon says, was "the first community act of thanksgiving in a permanent European settlement in what is now the United States"—a declaration that has gotten some New Englanders all in a lather. For their Florida feast, the Spaniards would have whipped up shipboard staples: salt pork, garbanzo beans, ship's bread (or hardtack), and red wine. The natives probably supplied the really good eating: seafood of all kinds, gleaned from coastal waters of the blue Atlantic.

But the first Floridians beat the Spanish *conquistadores* to the peninsula by thousands of years. People walked into the area that would eventually become metropolitan Orlando at least 12,000 years ago, archaeologists say. These Florida Paleoindians were descended from people who crossed into North America from eastern Asia during the Pleistocene epoch, the Ice Age. It's not clear exactly when these people made it across Beringia, the land bridge between the two continents as wide as the distance from Orlando to Manhattan, but it was before the Ice Age glaciers melted, argue archaeologists. After the meltdown, water covered much more of the globe, and the 1,000-mile–wide bridge between Asia and America disappeared, leaving the Bering Strait.

These early Floridians who arrived before the glaciers melted inhabited a peninsula unrecognizable to modern residents, scholars tell us. It was cool and arid rather than hot and humid, and it was about twice as large as the peninsula today. The spot on Florida's Gulf Coast where St. Petersburg sits, about 100 miles west of Orlando, would have been 50 miles inland in the Paleoindians' time, archaeologist Jerald T. Milanich writes.

The arid conditions meant a much different array of animals and plants than exists in modern Florida, and the resourceful Paleoindians made the most of it, turning every animal they could into food. These nomadic hunters dined on deer, fish, frogs, various turtles, freshwater shellfish, rattlesnakes, raccoons, opossum, rabbits, wood ibises, and panthers,

Milanich says. The Paleoindians also probably gathered a wide variety of plants as they moved from watering hole to watering hole. In the Orlando area, researchers have found spear points and other evidence of these prehistoric people near Lake Apopka, next to Shingle Creek in south Orange County, and at other sites.

When Spanish explorers landed on Florida's coasts in the sixteenth century, they encountered descendants of these earliest, nomadic Floridians who by now had added farming to their hunting and fishing. The ones we know the most about, in part because of the drawings of the artist Jacques le Moyne, are called the Timucua, a name given to them by the early explorers. Though they did not think of themselves as "tribes" in the sense we mean today, the Timucua, not the later-arriving Seminoles, constitute the closest thing to a native tribe for the northeastern and central areas of Florida.

It is true that Le Moyne's pictures and later engravings made from them offer a distorted view of the Timucua, seen through a European prism, but they also reveal much about these vanished people. They didn't wear much, sometimes only strands of Spanish moss, but they decorated themselves with jewelry and other body ornamentation. Men wore their hair in a topknot adorned with feathers or animal fur, historian Dana Ste.Claire writes. "Dyed fish-bladder ear plugs and long shell and bone pins were worn by both men and woman. Finely crafted jewelry was made of shell, bone, wood, stone and metal."

The Timucua people the Spanish encountered lived in fortified villages, surrounded by a palisade line or wall of sharpened, upright timbers, not unlike the forts United States soldiers would build to fight the Seminoles 300 years or so later. The Timucuan villages were much larger than Seminole war military stockades, though; a typical one contained about 30 houses and 200 to 300 people, as well as a central community house for political and spiritual ceremonies and activities.

By the time army soldiers were building their stockades, the Timucua were long gone, but not to lands in the West, where so many later American Indians would be forced to go. The descendants of the first Floridians had ceased to exist. For what the Europeans did not know when they arrived in the New World was that, along with their courage, drive, energy, greed, good intentions, and dreams, they brought death along with them.

Spanish missionaries had hoped to convert the Indians, but "microbes did not discriminate between Christian and non-Christians," as archaeologist Milanich has written. "Colonization was not kind to any of Florida's Indians." By 1700, the Timucua and other native Floridians had been decimated by bubonic plague, chicken pox, dysentery, diphtheria, influenza, malaria, measles, scarlet fever, smallpox, typhoid, typhus, and yellow fever, as well as by forced labor and raids by slavers. "By 1763, warfare, slave raiding and especially epidemics of disease had annihilated what had been a population of some 350,000 people at the time Ponce de Leon first came to Florida in 1513," Milanich writes.

Into the population vacuum left by these vanished native peoples on the Florida peninsula came the people who by the 1760s were being called the Seminoles. The name comes from a corruption of the Spanish word *cimarrones*, which means untamed and wild. Like so many settlers later in Florida, these people saw under its hot, sunny skies the prospect of a new life, free from the international and tribal wars being played out in the colonies north of Florida. Most of them were Lower Creeks from Georgia and Alabama who sought independence from the Upper Creeks. They heard of fertile land to the south, good for farming and raising livestock.

As they moved into Florida, these Creek immigrants were joined by scattered survivors of other indigenous people and by runaway slaves, some of whom had been captured in Africa from warrior tribes such as the Ibo and the Ashanti of the Gold Coast. By the time Florida became a U.S. territory in 1821, it had long served as an escape route for slaves from Georgia and South Carolina. Some of these freedom-seekers were able to sail from Florida ports to freedom in the Bahamas; others found homes with the Seminoles, who welcomed the warrior skills of their African-born allies.

During their two periods of rule (1565–1763 and 1783–1821), the Spanish encouraged the Seminoles' movement into Florida; they were eager to gain allies against their colonial rival, Great Britain, which controlled Florida in the 20-year gap in Spanish domain from 1763 to 1783 as part of the treaty that ended the French and Indian War. When the Spanish took over the second time in 1783, their long-distance, half-hearted colonial rule was no match for the boisterous expansion of the young United States.

Americans in the southern states coveted Florida and felt it "belonged to the United States as a foot belongs to a leg," historian John K. Mahon writes, and they didn't feel the same way the largely nonresident Spaniards had about the "untamed" natives and their African allies. They wanted Florida's land, and they also wanted to seek out and seize Africans and their children and restore them to slavery. "This is a Negro war, not an Indian war," one of the army's commanders, General Thomas S. Jesup, once told soldiers recruited to fight in Florida.

Historians divide the United States' conflict with the Seminoles and their black allies into three wars during the years 1817 to 1858: the first, while Spain still held Florida, largely in 1817 and 1818; the second and major one, from 1835 to 1842, and the third, about 1855 to 1858. But these can all be seen as part of one long struggle that began with the arrival of Europeans—what some historians have called not the settlement, but the invasion of America. In Florida, that struggle heated up around 1812 and lasted for more than 40 years.

In the Second Seminole War alone, which lasted seven years, the government waged the longest and costliest Indian war in the nation's history and was never able to conclude it with a peace treaty. At that conflict's end in 1842, less than 300 Seminoles remained in Florida of the nearly 5,000 who had once called the territory their homeland. More than 1,500 U.S. soldiers or residents had died in the effort to wrestle the land from the Seminoles. Still, some hung on and remained in the home their people had adopted.

Speaking to the U.S. House of Representatives in June 1842, the delegate from the territory of Florida, David Levy, argued that the Seminoles had no ancestral right to Florida:

> Sir, the sympathies of the public have been enlisted by the supposition that these Indians were about to be torn unwillingly from the hunting-grounds of their ancestors, and the graves of the past generations of their people. Nothing could be more mistaken. . . . No part of the Indians found in Florida at its cession were aborigines of that peninsula; and most of them were very recent refugees and stragglers from other parts.

ORLANDO

That was not how the Seminoles saw it. Also in the nation's capital, some years before Levy spoke, a delegation of Florida natives had gone to try to make their case to President John Quincy Adams. One of them, Tuckose Emathla, told of his people's deep connection to Florida. "Here our navel strings were first cut, and the blood from them sunk into the earth, and made the country dear to us," he said.

Like so many dwellers since, whose ancestors lived elsewhere, the Seminoles had found a home in the sandy land at America's edge, the deep-down peninsula where they had carried their dreams. It was from their fierce struggle to remain in their homeland that Orlando, the heart of Florida, was born.

Chapter Two

LEGENDS OF THE PALMETTO PRAIRIE

One of the most solid paeans to Orlando's roots in the Seminole wars perpetuates what is most likely a bit of make-believe enshrined in granite: a fitting monument for a city linked in the American mind to fantasy and imagination.

The monument was created with great sincerity, as such tributes are, by schoolchildren who saved their pennies for a noble cause. In 1939, the students of Orlando's Cherokee Junior High School pooled their change for the stone marker that still sits at the southeast corner of Lake Eola Park, the city's most venerable spot of public greenery. Lake Eola Park is to Orlando what Central Park is to New York, only much smaller. The walk around the lake is about a mile. On that stroll, you'll pass the marker, tucked below a tall pine. Here is what it says:

ORLANDO REEVES
In whose honor our city Orlando was named
Killed in this vicinity by Indians, September 1835
"How sleep the brave who sink to rest
By their country's wishes blest."

Across the lake sits a classy high-rise condo named Reeves House, and less than a mile away, a housing complex carries the name Reeves Terrace, both for the brave Orlando, hero of the Seminole wars. For a chap who almost positively never existed, this guy Reeves has carved a pretty good niche for himself in history.

By the time the junior-high children honored him in 1939, the valor of Orlando Reeves had been long enshrined in local legend. The story went back to a night in September 1835, according to the best retelling of the tale, set down in the 1930s by Orlando historian Kena Fries.

The September moon floated full above Sandy Beach Lake, now Lake Eola, when a company of soldiers stopped for the night, Fries writes. They quickly pitched camp and tethered and fed their ponies. "Coffee pots bubbled and frying pans sizzled."

The weary soldiers retired, except for one: Orlando Reeves, the sentinel, who paced the camp's perimeter in the bright moonlight. In the wee hours, he noticed a log rolling toward him. He rubbed his eyes, investigated, and spied more rolling shadows. But they were not logs, no indeed. They were the stealthy enemy creeping up on the sleeping camp. Without hesitation, Reeves sounded the alarm, knowing full well it meant death to him. He fell, "pierced by more than a dozen poisoned arrows," as Fries tells it, a martyr to "civilized" settlement of the area and the first recipient of Christian burial rites in the place that would bear his name.

The brave Orlando is remembered as a "tall, lanky young man, wiry and dark-complected." In Fries's version of the story, he was killed at Lake Eola but buried under a tall pine at nearby

Lake Lawsona. In another version, the soldier's compadres lay him to rest "under an oak tree on the south side of Lake Eola."

The story had great potential for patriotic embellishment, especially in days before history books included any mention of the Seminoles' side of the Seminole war story. "Beloved by all his comrades and feared by the Indians, Orlando could always be found where the fighting was the thickest," library director Olive Brumbach proclaimed in a 1929 retelling on local radio station WDBO. "Leading his comrades on to victory, Orlando Reeves made the supreme sacrifice upon the altar of patriotism in defense of his country's flag."

After investigations began in the 1970s, however, it seems pretty certain there was no Orlando Reeves. Federal military records are quite reliable, researchers say. He's just not there. Yet he has a perpetual life of sorts through his Lake Eola monument, reinforced in the city's imagination by the nearby statue of a Confederate soldier, gun ready on his shoulder, ever vigilant above the flower beds. And so, though he never existed, the stalwart sentinel lives on.

Like many legends, this one about a soldier killed by stealthy Seminoles bears elements of history's truth. The area that would become Orlando, Florida—America's vacation playground—did spring from the kind of wild-frontier warfare Americans usually associate with the Old West.

Florida's Seminole wars were not the stuff of sweeping prairie battles between war-whooping warriors and charging cavalry, however. Orlando's roots reach back instead to skirmishes on the palmetto prairie that were more like the jungle combat of Vietnam than the modes of war taught at West Point in the nineteenth century. The challenge of grappling with the Seminoles' hit-and-run tactics "can be properly appreciated only by those acquainted with them," wrote General Thomas S. Jesup, one of the army's commanders during the Second Seminole War.

The wet terrain made matters even worse. In those days, before the massive drainage projects that have by now converted acres of Florida from swamps to suburbs, the soldiers slogged their way through expanses of wetlands buzzing with mosquitoes. In fact, the first name for the sprawling area where Orlando would be located was Mosquito County.

Despite their environmental advantages, though, the Seminoles had problems of their own. By 1835, they fielded only 800 warriors to counter 5,000 regulars and militia available to fight them. Still, they managed to engage the United States in a frontier struggle as stirring, and as sad, as any in the country's history. It involved some tough customers on both sides. Looking around him, one militia recruit in the saga described his companions as "rough ungainly people . . . who look and act like the characters we read about in Coopers Indian novels as near as I can judge."

When General Jesup took command of the several thousand soldiers in Florida in 1836, things had not been going well for the army in its battle with the swamp-savvy Seminoles and their black allies. On December 28, 1835, Seminole warriors ambushed and killed all but three of 108 soldiers led by Major Francis Dade, near what today is Bushnell, about 50 miles from present-day downtown Orlando.

The attack had been planned by the daring Indian leader Osceola, the most famous of Florida's native people, thanks in part to his betrayal and capture in October 1837 by Jesup under a white flag of truce. After Osceola died a few months later of complications from malaria, Jesup's treachery helped make him a martyr and a legend, an image enshrined in the portraits well-known artists painted during his last days in prison. It didn't hurt that he was young, handsome, and charismatic. The great American painter George Catlin called him "an extraordinary character."

When Osceola died at Fort Moultrie, South Carolina, in 1838, he was the most famous Native American, his passing reported on front pages around the world. His mystique proved enduring and widespread. Danish author Karen Blixen, who later used the pen name Isak Dinesen when she wrote *Out of Africa*, wrote her first stories under the name Osceola. One of the counties in the Orlando metropolitan area, adjacent to Walt Disney World, bears the name, as does a national forest and scores of other public and private locales. Ironically, the warrior who fiercely resisted white policy, who was the most feared of his brethren, has "now become a white man's Indian by virtue of appropriation," anthropologist Brent Richards Weisman has written.

Osceola was feared for good reason; he was a killer for his cause. It was Osceola who ambushed and scalped federal agent Wiley Thompson, the man in charge of removing the Seminoles to the West, on the same day as the ambush of Dade's forces near Bushnell. That night, warriors celebrated both victories with a dance around the scalp of the hated Thompson, atop a 10-foot pole. About a month before, in a violent argument, Osceola had killed Charley Emathla, one of the Seminoles who had decided to accept the government's terms and leave Florida.

If you want to know Florida like a native, tuck away the fact that Osceola was not a chief; he was a guerrilla leader. The child born Billy Powell in Alabama in 1804 came to Florida with his mother as a refugee when he was about 10 after an 1814 treaty forced the Upper Creeks to give their Alabama lands to the United States. The boy's father was a British trader, William Powell; his mother, Polly Copinger, was a Creek whose ancestry also included Scottish and African strands.

Likely influenced by boyhood lessons from his great uncle, a powerful Creek leader named Peter McQueen, a teenage Billy Powell adopted his Indian name in a tribal ceremony about 1820. *Osceola* is actually an anglicized pronunciation of *Asi-yaholo*, which means something like Black Drink Crier or Black Drink Singer. *Asi* meant the dark, caffeine-rich tea brewed from yaupon holly and long used by Florida's native peoples in ceremony and war.

Osceola's fierceness was also fueled by personal tragedy, according to legends captured in Minnie Moore-Willson's 1896 book, *The Seminoles of Florida*. He had married a woman whose mother was descended from a fugitive slave, the story goes. One day when Osceola's wife accompanied him to the trading post at Fort King (now Ocala, Florida), white men seized her and carried her away in chains. "Osceola became wild with grief and rage, and no knight of cavalier days ever showed more valor than did this Spartan Indian in the attempts to recapture his wife," Moore-Willson wrote in the romantic style of her times.

If this story is not true, it has, like the legend of Orlando Reeves, the resonance of truth in it. Osceola vehemently opposed the surrender of runaway slaves, and much of his support came from blacks, historian James Covington writes in *The Seminoles of Florida*. During a raid on Osceola's headquarters in January 1837, soldiers took 55 prisoners, of whom 52 they classified as black and only three as Seminole.

Today, if you visit the Fort Moultrie National Monument in South Carolina, guides will show you where Osceola spent his last days. During a visit in the 1990s, Central Florida historian Jim Robison noted that postcards for sale at the fort declared Osceola had been buried with full military honors. If it is true, Robison says, military honors must involve the removal of one's head because, sadly, that's what happened to Osceola.

An army doctor named Frederick Weedon removed the warrior's head before burial and kept it as a souvenir in his St. Augustine drugstore. Stories passed down in the Weedon family say he would leave the head on the bedpost of children he thought needed discipline. After Dr. Weedon's death, his family gave the head to a New York surgeon, who gave it to the Medical College of the City of New York. A fire in 1866 destroyed the museum and its contents.

Lore from Orlando's early days linked Osceola and other Seminole leaders with a lost landmark for the city: the Council Oak, in its glory said to have been the largest live oak in southern Florida. "Here it is stated on what seems to be reliable authority," Indian strategists had planned the Dade ambush and "many other sudden attacks on the early settlers," Orlando's Kena Fries wrote in the 1930s.

The "authority" may have been the author's father, John Otto Fries, one of pioneer Orlando's most respected figures and a man who knew its landscape like no other. The Swedish son of a distinguished professor of botany at the University of Uppsala, Fries arrived in Orlando in late 1871 and brought his family in 1873. For many years he was surveyor for Orange County and later a U.S. surveyor. In 1900, he took the first official census of the remaining Seminole Indians in Florida, on their south Florida reservation.

It's a good bet that both J. Otto Fries and his daughter Kena had seen the Council Oak in its glory days. Sometime in the 1880s, it was struck down by lightning; a spectral version survives in photos from about 1910, when an observer noted that the bare ground around the trunk "indicated branches had spread over one acre." By then, vandals had chipped away at the ruin, turning it into fence posts and firewood. For Kena Fries, who died in 1945, the vanished giant was the spiritual core of "long, long ago" Orlando, and she treasured and pictured in her history of the city a fragment of the tree she had gleaned on an outing with a friend in 1904 and treasured for decades.

Gazing at the chip of oak, she wrote in the 1930s, she could close her eyes and forget the "swift high powered cars rushing along brick and asphalt highways, between miles and miles of the Golden Apples of the Hesperides"—groves of oranges. Under the Council Oak's spell, she could be transported to the days of Osceola and the heroic soldier Orlando.

By the twenty-first century, though, Miss Fries's icon of the past had vanished from the city's collective memory. One reminder remains: a marker much like the one to Orlando Reeves in Lake Eola Park. Placed by the Orange County Historical Commission in 1970, it sits unceremoniously in an Orlando neighborhood in the 1950s Florida style: low-slung homes of pastel concrete block surrounded by tropical trimmings. A vintage television antennae springs from the lawn a few feet away. "Nearby in the forest primeval, amid unfolding history," the marker reads, "once stood in majestic beauty the Council Oak, traditional meeting place of the Indian chiefs in the Seminole Indian War."

Like Reeves, the Council Oak may be pure folktale, but it's also a good possibility that Florida's native peoples did use the tree as a landmark, as they did for the giant cypress called the Senator that survives a few miles north in neighboring Seminole County. At more than 3,500 years old, the Senator remains one of the most venerable trees in America.

One of the best and brightest of the Seminole's leaders who, according to legend, met with other native leaders at the Council Oak had much stronger ties to the future Orlando area than Osceola. He was Coacoochee, the son of the Miccosukee chief King Philip, born in 1807 on an island in big Lake Tohopekaliga, south of Orlando. Army men called him Wildcat. Besides his father, he had other good connections: His uncle was Micanopy, the powerful head of the Alachua Seminoles farther north in the state.

At one point General Jesup captured Coacoochee under a flag of truce, as he did Osceola, but with different results. The general was enraged when the young chief escaped from the Spanish-built fortress at St. Augustine with nearly 20 other Seminoles. Later, soldiers kidnapped a small daughter of Coacoochee's and held her as a possible bargaining chip with the chief. He thought the child was dead, but at peace talks in 1841 she was released to him and came toward him "holding in her outstretched palms powder and bullets she had been able to collect and hide in captivity," John K. Mahon writes in his *History of the Second Seminole War*.

At the sight of his little daughter, the chief wept openly. But "his powers were not in the least weakened when it came to the talks," Mahon writes. Even the officers, fairly "hard of heart" when it came to their opponents, were moved by what Wildcat had to say. He loved the land of Florida, Coacoochee said.

> My body is made of its sands. The Great Spirit gave me legs to walk over it; hands to aid myself; eyes to see its ponds, rivers, forests and game; then a head with which I think. The sun, which is warm and bright as my feelings are now, shines to warm us and bring forth our crops. . . . The white man comes; he grows pale and sick. Why cannot we live here in peace? I have said I am the enemy to the white man. I could live in peace with him, but they first steal our cattle and horses, cheat us, and take our lands. The white men are as thick as the leaves in the hammock; they come upon us thicker every year. They may shoot us, drive our women and children night and day; they may chain our hands and feet, but the red man's heart will be always free.

In a bizarre bit of cosmic casting befitting Coacoochee's eloquence, observers noted he was dressed as Hamlet; beside him walked Horatio. The warriors had dressed in Shakespearean costumes from a theater troupe they had ambushed near St. Augustine months before. Along with the somber Hamlet, "others were ornamented with spangles, crimson vests, and feathers, according to fancy," an early historian noted.

It's likely, though, the Seminoles were motivated not by the urge to get fancy but just to have something to wear. Constantly on the move, they didn't have adequate clothes or food, and their plight worsened as their struggle went on, with women and children suffering the worst. "Some were reduced to wearing old corn sacks thrown away by the troops," John K. Mahon writes. At least once Indian women were seen picking up corn, kernel by kernel, that had been dropped accidentally by soldiers. Some students of Seminole history have said the traditional patchwork design of their clothing, now greatly prized, stemmed from the need to sew scraps together.

Although the soldiers had better garb, the "pale and sick" condition to which Coacoochee referred in his peace-talks address was not just rhetoric. This was not golf-course Florida;

army recruits from the North faced red bugs, fleas, horseflies, and mosquitoes, as well as what one soldier called "Florida fever," especially prevalent in the hot summers. More soldiers in the long fight against the Seminoles died from fevers, dysentery, severe diarrhea, and other illnesses than in battle.

Those suffering soldiers might be surprised to learn that decades later, legends link the United States military cry "Hooah!" with Coacoochee, one of their most formidable adversaries in the Florida wars. This is the exclamation made famous by Al Pacino's character in the movie *Scent of a Woman*. The story goes that during one peace summit, when various officers bellowed out toasts, including "Here's to luck," the fierce Coacoochee lifted his cup and exclaimed something like "hooah" in a deep, guttural voice.

About four years before he made his speech in the Hamlet costume, Coacoochee led an attack that would leave its mark on the Orlando area. At dawn on February 8, 1837, the young chief and his father, King Philip, led more than 200 other Seminoles in a raid on soldiers at Camp Monroe on the southern shore of Lake Monroe, part of the St. Johns River. A cannon on the steamboat *Santee* fired rounds to support the soldiers. After three hours of fighting, the camp's commander, Captain Charles Mellon, was dead and 15 more soldiers were wounded. The camp and the pioneer community that grew up around it (later Sanford) were renamed Fort Mellon to honor the slain captain.

Such attacks by Coacoochee and others inspired General Jesup to order the construction of a series of stockades roughly a day's ride apart that would boost the army's efforts and drive the war deeper into Seminole territory. Among them were Fort Gatlin, the origin of Orlando, and nearby Fort Christmas. We know more about the making of Fort Christmas than we do about Fort Gatlin, thanks to the journal of an army surgeon, Captain Nathan S. Jarvis, a copy of which is at Orange County's Fort Christmas Historical Museum. The museum, part of the county's parks system, also includes a full-scale recreation of the stockade and offers visitors a chance to imagine what these Seminole war forts were like.

Jarvis's descriptions help, too. Arriving in St. Augustine by steamboat in June 1837, he found a frontier society full of soldiers exhausted from fighting malaria as well as the elusive enemy. By mid-December, the doctor had joined troops who were deep in the Florida interior, where they passed deserted Seminole lodges. The enemy was also exhausted from always being on the run. Even in these bleak conditions, the Florida weather drew comments from a Northerner. December 22 was "delightful mild as September in the North," Jarvis wrote.

On Christmas Day, the soldiers reached their destination, a pine barren on what is now Christmas Creek. Using pine logs cut nearby, they began building a stockade 80 to 100 feet square, with four sides made of upright 18-foot pine logs, sharpened at the top. Inspired by the date, they named the place Fort Christmas. The soldiers had no tree or trimmings, of course, but a few days after Christmas, they did get a good meal when a scouting party of Alabama men turned up five cows. The rangy beef was far from filet mignon, but a welcome change from the soldiers' diet of salty dried meat and the occasional gopher tortoise. In just a few days, most of the troops were ordered to move on, deeper into Florida.

Ironically, the routes soldiers followed in their quest to master a wild land had been forged by their enemy, the Seminoles, or by earlier native peoples. Masters of the landscape, the Seminoles "traveled the shortest possible routes, as they knew where all the best crossings were in these muddy swamps," Myrtle Hilliard Crow wrote in *Old Tales and Trails of Florida*. In turn, the old Indian trails often followed paths forged by the real masters of the landscape, wild hogs and other animals.

These creatures followed the route of least resistance through boggy patches and swamps, crossing streams at the most practical places. "Low to the ground, compact and with plenty of weight behind them, wild hogs were nature's bulldozers," historian Mark Andrews has written. Decades later, many of the Orlando area's thoroughfares follow these old trails, carved by creatures and people who lived in deep kinship with the land. Even the concrete ribbon of Interstate 4 "roughly follows part of the old military trail that linked the sites of present-day Sanford, Orlando and Tampa," Andrews says.

One of these time-worn trails very likely followed the course west from Kena Fries's beloved Council Oak, rising first along what passes for a slope in the flat world of Florida and then dipping in curves between two lakes before it rises again to meet another lake. There, on a small triangular patch of high land between the three lakes today called Gatlin, Jennie Jewel, and Gem Mary, soldiers from Fort Mellon in late 1838 built the stockade that was Orlando's ground zero. They named it after an army surgeon, Dr. Henry Gatlin, one of the many killed in 1835 in the Dade ambush.

As soldiers had done at Fort Christmas, the men who built Fort Gatlin cut down tall, straight pines from the lakeside woods and lined them up into a square. They sharpened the top ends of the logs into points and built two-story blockhouses at diagonal corners. The inside courtyard of the stockade would be home to a storehouse, mobile cannons, and a powder magazine. About 3 feet off the ground on the inside of the log walls, the builders added a platform all around the perimeter. From there, riflemen would be able to fire at attackers through holes in the logs, although the Seminoles were too savvy to attack these forts directly.

Many of Florida's cities date from these Seminole war stockades, and some, such as Fort Myers and Fort Pierce, have retained their original names. A good many of them were occupied by soldiers very briefly, some for a matter of days, but as the conflict of the late 1830s transformed into the more peaceful years of the 1840s and settlement of Florida's interior began in earnest, these outposts offered safety for nearby settlers in case of Seminole uprisings.

One of Orlando's first pioneers, Martha Jernigan Tyler, left future generations a glimpse of what the Indian wars were like in handwritten memoirs, copies of which are in the archives of the Orange County Regional History Center. Her father was Aaron Jernigan, the cattleman and Indian fighter who is credited with being the first permanent settler in the Orlando area. Writing in 1913 when she was in her seventies, Mrs. Tyler tells of a harrowing night her family lived through in 1839, at Fort Moniac near the Okefenokee Swamp, before their move south into the Florida peninsula. Born February 14, 1839, she was only a few months old at the time; she recorded the story as she heard it from her mother. The quotes that follow reproduce her original spelling. On August 19, neighbors who had huddled together at Fort Moniac were attacked "between sunset and dark by the Seminole Indians." Mrs. Taylor wrote:

> . . . The first gun was fired, shooting cousen Eliza Patrick right through the root of her tongue, which happened a few minutes after sundown. [The mother of three small children, Cousin Eliza] looked at my father and tried to say "babie" enough

so that they knew what she had tried to say, so my Father went to the house where she was shot and got her babie to where she could see him.

Cousin Eliza died the next day at daylight. Mrs. Tyler's own mother, Mary Hogans Jernigan, was also shot, as was her 4-year-old brother Aaron, but both escaped serious harm. Mrs. Tyler wrote:

> When Father heared the first gun he told mother to run, which she did. She taken brother Moses in one arm and me in the other, and Father taken brother Aaron and his gun, and my sister, the oldest one of us, she run. She said she could hear the bullets whistle bye her head like hot tar from a torch.

Mary Jernigan was shot across the inside of her wrist and couldn't use her hand for six weeks, and her little boy Aaron was shot on his left elbow, Mrs. Tyler wrote. "Mother said his shirt sleeve was full of blood. She said she was afraid he would bleed to death before day light. The scar was there to his grave—he lived to be 76 years old."

Such episodes left scars of fear as well:

> My mother said she just motion her hand to us children and we would be quiete, so quiete you not known there was any children on the place. She was afraid of the Indians, oh yes. . . . The night of the 19 of August when they attacted us they whooped the Indian war whoop all night long and yelled to the top of their voices. Mother said it was enough to make the cold chills run over any one to hear their screams and shrill cries all night long. Sad indeed.

No attacks are recorded for the few months troops occupied Fort Gatlin, the seed of Orlando, about 185 miles south of Mrs. Tyler's Fort Moniac. Federal records indicate Fort Gatlin's main period of life as an army post was limited mostly to the months from early November 1838 to July 1, 1839, when it was occupied by various artillery units and dragoons (a kind of cavalry) and then evacuated. More than ten years later, during a period of fresh Seminole uprisings in the area, the fort was garrisoned again in the fall of 1849, according to army records.

But in spite of its short life as a working army post, the fort's pine logs had staked a place in the heart of Florida where a city could grow. By the time of its second and last occupancy, in 1849, a sprinkling of settlers had gathered near Fort Gatlin. Among them were Mrs. Tyler's family, the Jernigans, who would play a decisive role in making Orlando a place where newcomers did more than fight fevers and foes. They stayed on to plant and prosper.

Chapter Three

JERNIGAN, THE JUDGE, AND THE CRACKER KING

Pioneer Martha Jernigan Tyler could remember Orlando when more wolves roamed its woods than people. "We had plenty of varments such as bear tigers wolves wild cats and such like," she wrote in 1913, looking back on the 1840s and 1850s. "I have seen seven big wolves come right in front of the house about 2 o'clock and the sun a shineing bright and rase with their feet on a high log in a bout two hundred yards of the house and howl."

Mrs. Tyler's family, the Jernigans, faced wolves, wildcats, and warring Seminoles in a rough-and-rowdy land that was part old South, part wild West, and part raw Florida jungle. But the land offered good things, too. "We had fat deer and all we could use," she wrote. "Father bring five big fat Deer once, and other times big fat turkeys. When he would shoot them they were so fat they burst open on the breast." To go with the turkey, the family raised sweet potatoes, sugarcane, rice, corn, watermelons, muskmelons, and "pumpkins, world without end."

The father who brought home the fat of the land for his family, Aaron Jernigan, was a hero to his daughter, who called him "a brave soldier" in her memoirs. He was a father of sorts to Orlando as well. Along with the name of the Seminole war post Fort Gatlin, the first name to appear for the Orlando area on old maps is Jernigan. Historians credit Aaron Jernigan with being the first homesteader to put down roots and stick around. Except for descendants and historians, though, few present-day residents would recognize his name. In Orlando, you won't find a Jernigan High School, Jernigan Park, Jernigan Pumpkin Festival, or a Jernigan anything.

The founder, you see, left a troubled trail in the historical record that is almost schizophrenic. On one hand, he was a cattle baron, militia captain, and Orange County's first representative in the state legislature, in 1845. On the other, he was also a murder suspect, along with three of his sons, after a brawl at the Orlando post office in 1859 turned deadly. In its aftermath, Jernigan escaped from jail twice and took off for Texas, where he stayed for years while others built Orlando from a backwater settlement into a bustling boom town. The fatal post-office fight wasn't his only blot on history's pages. Before that case, his militia record "was reported to have been disgraceful," Seminole war historian James Covington notes. "During the past three months, he has been either drunk or sick (hangover)," one lieutenant recorded in 1856.

Perhaps the rigors of carving out a home on the jungle frontier were enough to drive a man to drink. Born in Camden, Georgia, Aaron Jernigan was just shy of 30 years old when he came with his brother Isaac to the middle of the Florida in the summer of 1843 to scout out his homestead. With him came an "old white gentleman" and two black men, almost certainly slaves, and his cattle—as many as 700 of them—according to his daughter Martha's memoirs.

Hundreds of cattle needed plenty of land, which is exactly what brought the brothers more than 185 miles south from their homes near the Okefenokee Swamp, about a year after the Second Seminole War had calmed down in 1842. On August 5, army officials reached an agreement with Chief Holata Mico, or Billy Bowlegs, whereby the 300 or so Seminoles who had not been killed or sent to the West would be allowed to remain in the southern part of the peninsula. To entice new residents into the territory of Florida, Congress had passed the Armed Occupation Act of 1842.

Come on down, build a cabin, defend it against any renegade Indians, cultivate five acres and stick it out for five years, and we'll give you 160 acres, the federal government said. Because the law's purpose was to pepper the land with white settlers, homesteads could not be less than 2 miles from a fort, a rule designed to keep settlers from huddling only around garrisons of soldiers.

The difficulties of the trip to Central Florida and the continued threat of Indian attack meant it took a hardy breed of pioneer to jump at the government's offer. The Jernigan family knew what the Indian wars could do; they had lived through the bloody attack at Fort Moniac in 1839, the year Martha Jernigan Tyler was born. But by 1843, the fierce Osceola had been dead for five years, and most of the Seminoles had been moved to the West. Maybe the Florida territory would offer them a new beginning. After filing his claim for land barely 2 miles from Fort Gatlin in July 1843, Aaron Jernigan went back to Georgia and, in January 1844, brought his wife Mary and their children to live in what was then sprawling Mosquito County. One of the children, Nathan, had been born just a month before.

Rather than bumping along the sandy paths forged from Indian trails, the Jernigans probably took the closest thing to expressway transportation in pioneer Florida: a steamboat traveling south up the north-flowing St. Johns River. The trip from Jacksonville to the wharf at Fort Mellon (modern Sanford), now a highway journey of less than three hours, took four days. A St. Augustine newspaper in 1842 described the lively scene at the dock as homesteaders began to infiltrate Florida's interior: "Just imagine children, dogs fighting, pigs squealing, geese quacking, turkeys gobbling, . . . some of the old women scolding, two or more fiddles screaking at intervals, and occasionally, steam blowing off."

From the wharf on the St. Johns, the Jernigans faced a journey of about 25 miles by wagon to their homestead near Lake Holden. When they arrived, their nearest neighbors were more than 20 miles away, back at Fort Reid, about a mile from the steamboat wharf. Eventually Aaron Jernigan would own about 1,200 acres in Central Florida.

About a year after the Jernigans arrived, in March 1845 the territory of Florida gained statehood. A couple of months earlier, in January, lawmakers had carved big Orange County from sprawling Mosquito County. Established in 1824, Mosquito had encompassed a huge swath of Florida. The original Orange County also was much larger than its later size, and included what would later become Seminole and Osceola. Aaron Jernigan was its first representative in the new state legislature.

In a letter in 1924, when she was in her 80s, Martha Tyler recalled another of her father's biggest contributions to pioneer days, when things had heated up again with the Seminoles in 1849. "The Indians were fussing and killing people around Tampa and Pease Creek, so father thought it best to build a fort," Mrs. Tyler wrote in a response to questions from Arthur T. Williams, president of the Florida Historical Society, whose own father had known Aaron Jernigan and visited the family's home.

When the fort was finished, "everybody went into it—altogether about 80 people besides the Negroes. We all stayed there about a year. The regular soldiers were forted about a mile west of us, altogether about three hundred of them. They left before we went home from the fort." Her father's stockade was near Lake Conway, Mrs. Tyler wrote. By building it, Aaron Jernigan had provided stability for the fledgling community around Fort Gatlin during unsteady times. Some of the settlers had panicked and left the area. Gathered together for a year, the pioneers in Jernigan's stockade found mutual support to stick it out and stay in Orange County.

Jernigan's daughter Martha had witnessed life in the stockade with the wide eyes of a child of ten. The only serious fight during the long year there involved "two old women" who "quarreled a half hour," she recalled. "One of them had a butcher knife and the other a fire stick, but they never got nearer than twenty or thirty feet of each other. One was Mrs. Marston and the other one Mrs. Lee."

By 1850, when the families left the stockade and returned to their homes, the Jernigans' place had been established as the center of the fledgling community. On May 30, 1850, it was granted a post office, named Jernigan, with Wright Patrick as first postmaster and Hannigan Patrick as the horseback mail carrier between Jernigan and Bartow, about 65 miles away. Each week, some member of the Jernigan family brought in the mail from Mellonville, the settlement growing up around Fort Mellon on the St. Johns.

As the 1840s gave way to the 1850s, other families ventured to the area that would become Orlando. Names including Holden, Patrick, Lee, Yates, Delaney, Hughey, Stewart, Barber, Self, Mizell, and more found their way into history's pages. About 1850, John Worthington opened the first log cabin and store at the site of present-day downtown Orlando, as Mrs. Tyler remembered it from visits a few years later:

> Well, I knew the first little log house that was ever built in Orlando out of pine poles with the bark on them. It was a bout twelve feet long and eight wide and I had to stoop to go in at the door and there was a counter on one side and a few cigar boxes set on it with some candie in them and box of tobaco and a barrel of whiskey in one corner, that was in 1856.

That same year, 1856, was a turning point for Orlando, with consequences no pioneer could have imagined. The pivotal event was over quickly—just a good old-fashioned picnic—but without it, a whole lot of things down the line would have shaped up very differently. It's a good possibility, for example, that folks visiting Walt Disney World would be riding re-creations of steamboats from the Jernigans' days at a frontier land on the St. Johns instead of shaking Mickey's hand more than 30 miles away from the big river.

When Florida became a state in 1845, Mellonville, the river town that would become Sanford, was Orange County's seat, but by 1856 several other communities were champing at the chance to become the place where people gathered to transact official business. It took a long time to ride or walk from place to place, and having the county seat near your home was a decided advantage. The main challengers to Mellonville were the Jernigan settlement and what would become Apopka, then called the Lodge because it was the home of the oldest Masonic Lodge in Central Florida, chartered in January 1856. An election to choose between the Lodge, Mellonville, Jernigan, and other hopefuls was set for the following October.

ORLANDO

The key player in the contest was a South Carolinian, James G. Speer, 36 years old when he arrived at Lake Jennie Jewel by Fort Gatlin about 1854. He represented a second wave of Central Florida pioneers, a different type of arrival than the rough-and-tumble Indian fighters such as Aaron Jernigan, who likely was off riding the range during that October 1856 election. Judge Speer, as he was later called, was not a veteran of the Indian wars; he was a cotton farmer and lawyer whose grandfather had been a Revolutionary War veteran. He became a judge, state lawmaker, and "staunch defender" of what was right who "would never buy success by compromising principle," professor William Blackman proclaimed in his 1927 history of Orange County.

That may be so, but the judge also knew how to make things happen with political creativity. A member of the federal Indian Removal Commission, Speer knew members of the militia who were 21 or older could vote in any district in Florida where they happened to be on election day. Fort Gatlin had been abandoned in 1849, so there were no soldiers there, but Speer was undaunted. He headed to Sumter County and invited soldiers there to visit Jernigan for a fine election day feast, and they answered the call. The soldiers arrived in the morning, ate, and obligingly voted for the county seat to be moved to Jernigan. Mellonville on the river was out of luck.

It's not exactly clear what Speer's stake in the matter was. Ironically, the 1860 census shows him as a resident of Mellonville, the place he outmaneuvered four years before, and he later lived in west Orange County. Throughout its history, Orlando seems to have benefited time and again from people who stepped forward and went to bat for it, sometimes with obvious motivation and sometimes more mysteriously, at least as far as recorded history shows. You would almost think there was something magical in the water of the many lakes or in the silvery-green palmetto woods.

Perhaps Judge Speer thought so. Besides his role in making the place the county seat, he seems to bear prime responsibility for its final choice of name. In September 1857, less than a year after the soldiers' picnic election, the post office at Orange County's new seat officially transformed its identity. The place that had been Fort Gatlin, and then Jernigan, would now be Orlando, a name that doesn't sound much like a haven for Cracker cowboys. Where the heck did they get *Orlando*? It's one of the central puzzles in the city's past.

The city's official version embraces the story of a soldier named Orlando Reeves, killed by stealthy Seminoles near Lake Eola in 1835. But when local researchers, including librarian Eileen Willis, dug into federal War Department records in the 1970s and 1980s, they found no Orlando Reeves in the thorough records of the territorial militia or regular army in that era.

In 1975, Donald A. Cheney, then chairman of the county historical commission, wrote out his version of the name story for the *Orlando Sentinel*. Cheney, also a judge, was the son of Judge John Cheney, an 1885 arrival to Orlando and one of its prime movers and shakers. Judge Speer was a "gentleman of culture and an admirer of William Shakespeare," Cheney wrote. "According to him, this area was a veritable Forest of Arden, the locale of *As You Like It*," the Shakespeare play of which Orlando is the hero.

There's more to the story. If the Indian fighter Orlando Reeves is a figment of folklore, there did live in the mid-nineteenth century a man named Orlando Savage Rees, a planter from South Carolina who also owned large estates in Florida and Mississippi. In 1955, F.K. Bull of Pinopolis, South Carolina, told an Orlando reporter he "had been brought up on the story" that the city of was named for his great-grandfather, Orlando Rees. Years later, Charles M. Bull Jr. of Orlando also offered historians information about Orlando Rees, his great-great-grandfather.

In an 1832 diary entry, John James Audubon mentioned meeting Orlando Rees at his gracious home at Spring Garden, about 45 miles from present-day Orlando. A few years later, in 1837, Rees wrote from his Charleston, South Carolina home to federal authorities in Washington, asking the government not to conclude a peace treaty with the Seminoles unless the deal included the return of slaves the Indians had taken, or compensation for the losses. Orlando Rees apparently was among the sugar-growing planters who had been burned out of the area by Seminole attacks in late 1835 (the year of the fictional Orlando Reeves's death). One story says Rees led an armed expedition to recover his stolen slaves and cattle. His route might have taken him through what is now downtown Orlando.

On his ride, Rees could have left a pine-bough marker with his name on it next to the military trail, researchers have suggested. Early memoirs talk of a tree bearing such a mark. Travelers might later have seen the sign, mistakenly read it as "Reeves," and assumed it was a grave marker. The real Orlando wasn't buried in Florida, though. He died back in South Carolina in 1852 at the age of 58.

Whether by association with the planter Orlando Rees or the mythical soldier Orlando Reeves, stories of a spot called "Orlando's grave" took hold. Pioneer William B. Hull, who was at the 1857 meeting to name the new county seat, told family members the debate had grown hot and heavy when the influential Judge Speer rose and said, "This place is often spoken of as 'Orlando's Grave.' Let's drop the word 'grave' and let the county seat be Orlando."

Speer's descendants are firm in their belief, though, that the judge's true motive was his fondness for Shakespeare, and that he had in mind the Orlando of *As You Like It*, set in the Forest of Arden. It's certainly plausible that the good judge would be well versed in Shakespeare; during his era, the works of the Bard were standard public-school reading, as they continued to be well into the twentieth century.

Whatever the reasons, the village called Jernigan became Orlando in 1857, and its locus shifted a few miles from the Fort Gatlin area to the homes around John Worthington's store—what is now downtown Orlando. The year before, in 1856, military officials had relieved Aaron Jernigan of his militia command, after complaints about rowdy conduct by Jernigan's company of volunteers. "It is said they are more dreadful than the Indians," Secretary of War Jefferson Davis noted in a June 1856 letter.

Jernigan's successor as prime pioneer, Judge Speer, again helped cast the die for the future by offering a site for the new county seat's courthouse. Speer was the attorney for B.F. Caldwell, an Alabama businessman who had acquired a good amount of land in the Orlando area. In a deed dated October 8, 1857, Caldwell donated 4 acres for the courthouse. A few days before his gift, he had sold all his other holdings in the area for $5.

Visitors to present-day Orlando can clearly see the location of Caldwell's courthouse site. Called Heritage Square, it's the park by the 1927 courthouse that now houses the Orange County Regional History Center, and the surrounding land. "It is from this site that the city limits of Orlando—originally one and one-half miles square—were first platted," an engraved stone at the square says. The first courthouse on the site was not built for another six years after 1857, though. The very first courthouse in Orlando was a log cabin with dirt floors on nearby Church Street. In 1863, it was replaced by a two-story log building at the Heritage Square location.

Two years after Caldwell's bequest, Aaron Jernigan almost lost his place in history. With three sons, Lewis, Moses, and Aaron Jr., Orlando's founder was involved in a brawl at the post office in 1859, and a man named William Wright was killed. The Jernigans turned themselves in, expecting a ruling of self-defense, but a jury gave them a nasty surprise when it indicted them, along with William Tyler, the elder Jernigan's son-in-law, and another man, Eli Prescott. Because Orlando had no jail, Judge Benjamin Putnam ordered the prisoners to Marion County, about 80 miles north in Ocala. On their 13th day of custody there, the four Jernigans broke out, the Ocala newspaper reported. The father was recaptured and spent about a year in jail in Ocala. Then, as the newspaper reported, the elder Jernigan "again became weary of confinement . . . and very unceremoniously left." There was some suspicion he had help in making his escape.

Jernigan went to Texas for 25 years but eventually returned to the community his name had put on the map and died there in 1891. The 1859 indictment and jail escape likely squelched any remaining chance he had of being lauded as a founding father in Orlando's early days. Professor Blackman's 1927 history of Orange County is lavish in its praise of other settlers, including Speer—lauded for his "Christian character"—but Jernigan gets scant mention.

Thanks to daughter Martha's memoirs, though, and to research years later by Central Florida historians including Brenda Elliott of Kissimmee, Jernigan is receiving belated recognition. "You have to look at what the frontier was," Elliott says. "It was a no-man's land . . . very rough and tumble, unsettled and primitive, dog-eat-dog, survival of the fittest." The stockade Jernigan built to protect settlers during the Seminole uprisings in 1849 was crucial. "Orlando owes an incredible debt that Jernigan came here and stuck it out until that next wave [of settlers] came through" in the 1850s.

Jernigan is buried in Lake Hill Cemetery, west of downtown Orlando. In 2003, residents who care for the old cemetery complained publicly about repeatedly finding the carcasses of dead chickens in the burial ground. Some residents theorized the remains were linked to voodoo rituals practiced by recent Caribbean immigrants to the neighborhood. Others thought the birds might have something to do with the cockfights long associated with that part of Orange County. The bloody dead birds had nothing to do with Jernigan's grave, but their presence hints that the wild land he settled still has a touch of wildness left in it. The Indian fighter who slashed through the swamps and brought home those fat deer his daughter Martha remembered might smile at the notion.

Jernigan's jail escape and flight to Texas came on the eve of the Civil War, a watershed period in American history, but one in which Central Florida did not play a major role. Orange County's population had almost doubled in the decade after 1850, but residents remained scarce: In 1860, the county's total was still less than 1,000 people in an area that today encompasses not only Orange but also Seminole, Lake, and Osceola Counties and parts of Brevard and Volusia as well. Recovering from the Seminole wars, the last of which ended in 1858, most Central Floridians were more concerned with the day-to-day problems of living than they were with secession politics. When forced to take a stand at a meeting on secession in Tallahassee, Orange County sent delegate William Woodruff, a staunch Unionist. He was one of the few who refused to vote to leave the United States in the conference's final 62–7 ballot for secession on January 10, 1861.

The war years brought little excitement but considerable poverty to Orlando. Federal blockades of ports and rivers cut supply lines into the South, Florida included, and residents scrambled to raise their own food and devise other necessities of life in the small community. The central settlement was tiny; besides the log court house, completed in 1863, downtown Orlando in Civil War days boasted only a couple of houses, two stores, and a saloon. Cornbread, grits, and sweet potatoes were the staples of the war-time diet. "To eat we got potatoes and a little milk," an Orlando woman wrote her soldier husband in 1864. "I have got some corn planted and there's peas and corn near the house and it looks very well."

The settlement's official post office had been closed in March 1861, but Mrs. William Hull continued to act as the unofficial postmistress while her husband was away at war. The couple had moved near the courthouse in 1860 and opened a boarding house close to present-day 47 South Orange Avenue, on what would become a major commercial block. An 1855 arrival to Orlando, James Hughey (the county's first clerk of the court), drove a mule team twice a month to Gainesville, still connected to supply routes by the Florida Railroad. He journeyed more than 100 miles each way to bring back provisions for his neighbors. Travel was hard for everyone. Freed from a Union prison in June 1865, William B. Hull was sent by boat from New York City to Palatka; he had to walk the 100 miles south to Orlando, where he arrived in July.

Weary and ragged, returning veterans such as Hull found a new era in Orlando in 1866, when Confederate forces in Florida officially surrendered. The end of the war marked a fresh beginning of inestimable importance for the area's African-American residents, now freed from slavery. "The slave population was never large in the area," however, as Leroy Argrett Jr. writes in his *History of the Black Community of Orlando*. Although Reconstruction supposedly brought the vote to black residents, whose numbers would increase in later decades, it would be many years before African Americans achieved true voting rights in Orange County. Not long after the Civil War, newly freed blacks in Orlando received bitter lessons if they tried to exercise their right to vote. According to Bacon's history, "on one occasion, 40 Negroes came in [to Orlando] to vote, but were whipped out of town by one Jack Ramey." The Reconstruction sheriff, David Mizell, "had a vicious fight on his hands" trying to arrest Ramey, but he managed to do so.

If it seems impossible for one man to drive away 40 others with a whip, consider that the weapon Ramey wielded was an impressive instrument in the hands of a Florida cow hunter, one experts could use with frightening speed and sound (Ramey probably didn't attack all 40 potential voters at once, either). Cracker cowboys in the dense palmetto prairie couldn't use lariats to round up cattle; a rope would have just joined the tangle. Aided by cattle dogs and nimble ponies that could negotiate scrub land and swamp, Florida range riders used bullwhips with a skill that could bring down a bird in flight, kill a rattlesnake, or turn a stampede. Florida folklore maintains that the loud crack of the whips was the source of the name Cracker, although it's likely the term is far older, with origins in England.

Range wars between factions of these whip-cracking cattlemen kept Orlando as wild and woolly during the Reconstruction years (1865–1877) as it had been during the Seminole wars, even without the Seminoles. In 1868, the log courthouse in Orlando—the one built in 1863 on the land Judge Speer's client had donated—was burned in an arson fire on the eve of the trial in a sensational cattle-rustling case. Bucket brigades of Orlandoans in nightclothes tried to save the courthouse, but it burned to the ground, and almost all the county's early records vanished in ashes. Sheriff David Mizell, the same fellow who stopped Jack Ramey's whip rampage, got the fall term of circuit court going soon in temporary quarters, but he faced an uphill battle. "Armed cattlemen and cowboys stood around the makeshift courtroom and glared at public officials," historian Jim Bob Tinsley writes. "Not one of them would testify against the other."

In early 1870, Sheriff Mizell himself became one of the most visible victims of the range wars when he was ambushed and shot to death out in cattle country, possibly trying to collect a debt from cattle baron Moses E. Barber. Judge John Mizell, the sheriff's brother, organized a posse, kicking into high gear a long-simmering feud between the Barber and Mizell families. Exactly how many were killed in the full-scale range war that followed isn't clear, but most historians of the saga tally at least nine, including Mizell, in less than three months. The most dramatic death seems to have been that of the younger Moses Barber, Moses Sr.'s son. When would-be avengers captured Moses Jr. at Orlando's Lake Conway, they rowed him out to the middle of the lake, tied a heavy plowshare around his neck and rolled him overboard. It looked as though he might make it to shore anyway, so they shot him. Memories of the Barber-Mizell feud continued to raise blood pressures in Central Florida well into the twentieth century.

The Reconstruction-era cattle wars in the Orlando area reached a high point after an immense rainstorm in 1871 destroyed all crops, and cattle raising remained as the chief means of livelihood. "The result was characterized by a complete disregard for law," Eve Bacon's history of Orlando states.

> Out of 41 murder indictments only 10 cases were heard and no guilty verdicts were returned. This breakdown of the courts made Orlando a brawling, frontier cattle town that would put a western movie to shame. . . . The actual number of people killed will never be known, as swamps, sink holes and lakes tell no tales.

Even if its lakes hid awful secrets, the Orlando landscape began to lure other settlers after the Civil War who would smooth the town's rough edges—more families "of education and culture," as Bacon's history puts it. No one had a better pedigree than Francis Eppes, Thomas Jefferson's favorite grandson, who moved to the area with his family from Tallahassee in 1868. They settled south of town on Lake Pineloch, not far from the location of Fort Gatlin in the 1840s. Three Eppes daughters had married brothers named Shine in 1866, and two of the couples followed Francis and Susan Ware Eppes to Central Florida.

Eppes' son-in-law T.J. Shine became a director of the First National Bank and commander of the Orlando Guard, which he organized and led. In 1879 he built a home surrounded by pine trees where two roads intersected. Shine cleared the trees and named the streets: The north-south passage became Orange Avenue, modern Orlando's main street, and the east-west one was Jefferson Street, after his wife's great-grandfather. The T.J. Shine home was considered a showplace. Orlando's first sidewalk ran in front of it, and it had a tennis court and Orlando's first bathroom, with water pumped from a well in the backyard. Five years after the Eppes and Shine families arrived, in 1873, Orlando gained a resident who towered over others in reputation and resources: Jacob Summerlin, the cattle king of Florida.

Jernigan, the Judge, and the Cracker King

According to legend, Summerlin was the first recorded child to be born as a U.S. citizen in the territory of Florida after it was acquired from Spain. Born in 1820 in the village of Alligator near Lake City, he built his first herds of cattle by selling 20 slaves given to him by his father. By the 1850s, he owned vast herds in what are now Orange, Osceola, and Polk Counties and beyond, to southwestern Florida. The Spanish paid him with saddlebags filled with gold coins for the cattle he sent in ships bound for Cuba. In years when some cattlemen were known by tales of wild escapades, Summerlin was known as a benefactor of folks in need. During the Civil War, it was said he branded some of his cattle "W" for widows and "O" for orphans and gave them away accordingly. Other stories said he would repay the hospitality of people who helped him on his travels by leaving hidden stacks of Spanish gold behind.

In 1873, Summerlin and his family moved to Orlando because it was a county seat near the center of his ranching empire. He bought 200 acres including Lake Eola, the present-day site of Orlando's central city park, for a reported price of 25¢ an acre. He built a grand home near Lake Eola that eventually became a hotel, Orlando's Waldorf-Astoria of its day. Despite depictions of Summerlin as a rough-hewn rustic trailing dust from his boots, Bacon's history of Orlando says he was really "a quiet, courteous, kindly person, but one who could be tough when the occasion demanded." And get tough he did, in 1875—not with fists or guns or his bullwhip, but with the power of all that Spanish gold he had acquired.

Summerlin liked his lake and his hotel and his new town just fine, and he wasn't keen on the idea of moving the county seat. It seems Judge Speer's machinations about 20 years earlier had not finally settled the matter, because that's exactly what General Henry Sanford wanted to do, move the county seat back to the St. Johns River. Sanford came to Orlando touting the growing town that bore his name, the new incarnation of Mellonville on the big river. He met with county commissioners at the 1869 frame courthouse that had replaced the earlier, arson-destroyed log structure. Built for $1,250, the 1869 courthouse was soon outgrown, and a new one was badly needed.

Sanford, the former U.S. minister to Belgium, wore a high silk hat and carried a gold-tipped cane, no Cracker bullwhips for him. But the dandy's offer was formidable. In a high-flown speech picturing all the glories to come in his new town, he offered to give free land for a new courthouse near the St. Johns River, the state's major thoroughfare.

Summerlin was in the packed crowd for the performance, and when it was over, he rose to his feet and asked Sanford if he was finished talking. "I have," came the curt reply. The king of cattlemen said:

> Then I will make my offer. The county seat has been located here by the free will of the majority of the settlers; the land has been deeded to that particular purpose. I stand here, ready to build a $10,000 court house, and if the county is ever able to pay me back, all right. If it can't, that's all right, too.

That took the wind out of Sanford's silk-hatted sails, and the county seat stayed put, solidifying Orlando's future. The county did pay Summerlin back his $10,000, but it took ten years to do it.

The year of the Summerlin-Sanford courthouse duel, 1875, marked another major turning point for Orlando. The city was incorporated that year, at a meeting in which William J.

ORLANDO

Brack swept a whopping 21 of the 22 qualified electors to become the first mayor of the city of about 85 souls. The same year, in December, Orlando gained its first newspaper, the Orange County *Reporter*. The staff consisted of three people, who acted as editors, pressmen, typesetters, reporters, advertising sales agents, and even newsboys when necessary. The presses for the paper had been dragged by ox cart over sandy roads from Mellonville and were set up in a wooden building at East Central and Main Streets.

Having struggled through the Civil War and Reconstruction, Orlando was on the move. It had grown to more than 200 people when one of Mayor Brack's early successors, Cassius A. Boone, took over in 1882. By then, the county that had numbered less than 1,000 in 1860 had grown to more than 6,600. The engine powering the growth was exactly that, or more precisely, a railroad: the South Florida Railroad, which officially arrived in Orlando on October 2, 1880, to much gala celebration.

The previous January, former President Ulysses S. Grant had inaugurated the line by turning the first spade of earth in ceremonies at Sanford. As the inaugural train chugged toward Orlando in October, it was accompanied by explosive merriment. On the last car "some of the more boisterous members of the party had mounted a cannon," Bacon's history says. When the engine stalled several times during the trip, the more energetic folks on the train would jump off, push it onward and then scramble on board and fire the cannon.

At their destination, the noisy celebrants were treated to some good eating. Two large tables had been set below pine and live oak trees near what is now Orlando's main downtown intersection. One was reserved for the African-American laborers who had actually built the line. "The laborers applied the same expediency to the food as they used in building the road," Bacon writes. "They had been living on commissary rations and were enjoying their first real meal in months."

The rail link to main transportation routes gave Orlando what it needed to blossom. Settlers had been experimenting with citrus for some time, and the area was gaining a reputation as a place to grow oranges, but without the railroad, Orlando lacked a way to get the fruit to market before it spoiled. Soon, the cattlemen who had ruled Central Florida would be getting some competition from new arrivals eager to turn the sweet orange fruit into green dollars.

The cattle barons were still much in evidence, however. In May 1883, Jacob Summerlin came to Orlando's city council and offered to donate to the city a strip of land around Lake Eola on the condition that it be beautified and made into a park. He stipulated that the city should plant trees and put a driveway around the lake. As always, the Cracker king knew how to take care of business; reverter clauses in this final gift stated that if the city's obligations weren't met, Summerlin's heirs could reclaim the property, which they made noises about doing a few years later. The city fathers got busy planting trees and filling in marshy spots, and Lake Eola remained Orlando's.

Summerlin's 1883 gift established Lake Eola—the place where Orlando Reeves had roamed in the city's folklore—as a hub around which the city would grow, and many years later, a street close to the lake still carries the name of Summerlin, the very real Florida legend who made certain the seat of Orange County stayed right where he wanted it.

Chapter Four

HOT AND COLD TIMES
IN THE PHENOMENAL CITY

The coming of the railroad to Orlando in 1880 meant its days as a true pioneer town were numbered. Sure, Cracker cowboys could be seen on its streets for years to come. But with rail and steamboat transportation linking the little city to the rest of the country, one no longer needed the grit of a Jernigan or the resources of a Summerlin to take a look at what Orlando was all about and decide to stay awhile. Newcomers could build a home by a lake, plant oranges, say goodbye to cold and snow forever. Under sunny skies and mossy oaks, the strictures and structures of society seemed to bind less tightly. Orlando was a good place to reinvent yourself or just take your personal show to a new, brighter stage.

And so it was no longer mostly from Georgia or South Carolina that new residents appeared on Orlando's streets. They came from the North and from the Great Plains and even from Europe, especially from England, where folks long have shown a special fondness for Florida. It wasn't the Empire, it's true, but perhaps their empire-building experience had taught Englishmen a thing or two about setting out to see what the wide world had to offer. Orlando had plenty, its boosters proclaimed.

Mahlon Gore came from Iowa to stake his claim to a new life in the sunshine early in 1880, just a few months before rail service began. The experienced newsman bought the Orange County *Reporter*, and in June published the first issue with his name on the masthead. When he arrived, the entire business district was on three sides of the courthouse square, at what is now Central Boulevard and Magnolia Avenue.

"There were four stores, one hotel, one blacksmith and wagon shop and a livery stable," Gore wrote. At the stable, customers had to leave their order for a conveyance two days in advance, to give the liveryman time to go out into the woods and hunt down a horse. But the South Florida Railroad connection had transformed the place. Soon "five sawmills and two planing mills began to turn out lumber, and a building boom was on. In four years there were 41 mercantile establishments and three livery stables."

The building boom was going so strong that it was able to recover from a major blow in January 1884: the worst fire in the young city's history. Much of the business district was destroyed by the blaze that started in James Delaney's grocery store at East Pine and Main (Magnolia) Streets. Two clerks sleeping on the second floor of the building were awakened by the smoke between 4:00 and 5:00 a.m. and sounded the alarm. The offices of Gore's *Reporter* were almost completely destroyed, but he showed his mettle by making arrangements with the *Sanford Journal* 25 miles away to get his paper out. The *Reporter's* "fire edition" of January 17, describing the holocaust, brought Gore a cash reward from other business leaders and $300 in new subscriptions.

Orlando's volunteer firefighters fought the blaze admirably, containing it with explosives that kept the flames from destroying absolutely every building in the business district, but the 1884 conflagration was serious proof that the city needed something more. On July 4, 1885, Orlandoans celebrated the arrival of their first fire truck, and R.L. Hyer loaned the new Orlando Hook and Ladder Company two horses to pull it around town to show it off, while members of the old volunteer department followed with the hose and reel. The party ended with a banquet at the Opera House, built after the big blaze in 1884.

Several months after the fire, newsman Mahlon Gore commissioned a census of Orlando, which he published in the *Reporter* for August 14, 1884. The population was 1,666, Gore said: 698 white men, 464 white women, 280 African-American men, and 224 African-American women. Four years earlier, the total had been a mere 200. By 1886, Orlando was touting itself as the "Phenomenal City." "The growth of Orlando is phenomenal, as there are no oil wells, factories or mines," a South Florida Railroad brochure proclaimed. Instead the little city depended "entirely on its orange groves, truck gardens and unrivaled climate. Orlando is built on the peel of an orange."

Soon the city's new daily newspaper, the Orlando *Record*, declared itself a "phenomenal daily published in a phenomenal city." Wanton S. Webb's 1886 business directory also picked up the "phenomenal" theme and claimed 3,528 for the city's population—which, if true, is more than double Gore's figure of 1,666 tallied a couple of years before.

The blooming city wasn't built so much on the peel of an orange as it was on efforts to sell land to potential orange growers. "The tenderfoot on arriving here sees nothing but business," Webb's directory declared. On Pine Street, the visitor would find himself in the thick of things, the site of the "real estate exchanges which have done so much for and made the city so famous. . . . An air of business seems to be breathed by all." The real estate men had horses and "expensively caparisoned turnouts" (buggies, one assumes) at the ready to carry visitors out into the surrounding country for a look-see. The land that settlers such as Aaron Jernigan had claimed for free about 40 years before was now a commercial commodity. And some of the new arrivals to the Phenomenal City crossed an ocean to own it.

A few Englishmen such as future Orlando hardware merchant Joseph Bumby had arrived in town before the boom, moved by their own initiative and self-sufficiency to take up the pioneering life in Florida. Many in the wave of 1880s arrivals from England heard a different call, however. English investors who had scooped up large tracts in Central Florida for about a dollar an acre placed ads in British papers picturing the easy life of a gentleman citrus grower in Florida, the new Utopia. With claims of a "certain annual income of at least $10,000 after the groves had reached maturity," the ads proved effective. One focus of British settlement was Lake Conway, not far from the site, years earlier, of Aaron Jernigan's stockade. About 1885, English arrivals organized a Yacht Club and had boat races on the lake for more than 10 years.

The whole episode "seems typically British to my mind, particularly for that period," says Peter Stanhope, an Englishman who owns a vacation home in Central Florida and has studied Orlando's English colony in the 1880s. The speculators found a "lucrative source of investment from the landed gentry of Britain," who sent their younger sons out to seek their fame and fortune, Stanhope says. "The first sons were secure because they would inherit the estates, the aristocratic homes, lands and so forth—that's what first sons did." The other sons got nothing. So it seemed a good idea for them to head off to some imagined Utopia such as Florida to make a name for themselves, fueled by a monthly remittance to keep them going until they settled in. "They became known as remittance men because they were always waiting for the next check to come through the mail from daddy back home," Stanhope says.

Tales from Blackman's history of Orange County detail the shock of sons of the gentry confronting the Florida frontier. One group of young arrivals returned to their Kissimmee hotel and, "running true to English form, placed their shoes outside the door to be polished," Blackman wrote. "Much to their disgust," they found the shoes "in the morning where they had left them, untouched, and were assured by the young English clerk that they were 'jolly lucky' to find them at all."

Some, like Captain Dudley G. Cary-Elwes, had the right stuff. Born in 1837, he was well past the idealism of youth. Cary-Elwes had served with Her Majesty's Third Infantry in Corfu in 1857, India in 1858, and China in 1859–1861 before he headed to Florida with his family more than 20 years later. At their large home on what is now Lake Fredrika, they "entertained liberally," according to Blackman's history. Instrumental in the building of the Orlando Protestant Episcopal Church, the former colonial soldier later moved into the city, where he and his wife both died in 1914.

Perhaps his years in India and China had prepared Cary-Elwes for life in Florida, but many young English folks were surely strangers in a strange land. Judge T. Picton Warlow, who arrived from England in 1884 and stuck it out to later become a city eminence, recalled some of the highs and lows in his 1937 memoirs:

> These Englishmen suffered from intolerable loneliness. Imagine if you can, a young man on a hot, wet night in September, sitting down at a bare table, writing a letter home, wearing high boots and a macintosh with the collar turned up to protect him from gallinippers and mosquitoes—for they were voracious in those days—and then having a small, gentle green tree frog, which had entered under the eaves, flop down on the page of the letter he was writing.

It's likely not many of the young gents expected to actually do the orange growing themselves. In the English community at Narcoossee in southeast Orange County, Warlow wrote, the settlers characteristically built their tennis courts first, much to the surprise of the "hard-headed American nurseryman who afterward set out their orange groves."

Pleasures such as a good game of tennis eased the pain of separation from home. "Hunting in winter, tennis all year around, and other sports, finally golf, relieved the monotony of life," Warlow wrote, and with more winter visitors and new settlers, social life began in earnest. Especially gracious hosts were the Leslie Pell-Clarkes, wealthy northeasterners who had arrived in Orlando in the 1880s and bought a big house on North Main Street. They "kept open house," Warlow wrote, "and were probably the most hospitable people who ever came to Orlando." One winter "two utterly entrancing young ladies from Atlanta visited the Pell-Clarke home, the Misses Willie and Jessie Reed, and the house immediately became the center of activity."

When Leslie Pell-Clarke wasn't entertaining, he was often outdoors giving his bicycle a whirl, on the cyclists' path he had built around the north side of Lake Eola. It headed east over the sand hills near the later site of Orlando High, now Howard Middle School, and continued over a rustic bridge across Fern Creek and down woodland trails to the polo grounds (near present-day Harry P. Leu Gardens), a major focus of the English colony's sporting and social life in the 1880s and 1890s. Pell-Clarke's enthusiasm for cycling was shared by members of the Orlando Bicycle Club, who organized their first official race in 1895.

English settlers in search of entertainment could also head to the English Club on Main Street at East Pine. Built in 1886–1887 by Englishman Gordon Rogers and other investors, the two-story frame structure is one of the city's few Victorian survivors and, with the Bumby Hardware building, one of the two oldest commercial buildings in Orlando. Part of the downstairs was originally a carriage house. The section closest to the corner housed a pub called the Cosmopolitan Club, a gents-only establishment. Ladies had to use an exterior staircase to reach the large social hall upstairs—the scene of many festive occasions, "when the debonair Britishers gathered for dances, theatricals, cards, and other social activities," Bacon's history says.

In its long life, the Rogers Building has had many, varied tenants. During the early 1900s, after the English Club disbanded, the Reverend Nellie Cherry conducted First Spiritualist Church ceremonies in the upstairs social hall. Much later, in the 1950s, that space was home to an Arthur Murray Dance Studio. Downstairs, six restaurants passed under the old pub's pressed-tin ceiling during the twentieth century. The last, the Landmark, closed in 1983. Juries from the nearby county courthouse would often dine there, among them the sequestered jury for the 1979 trial of famed serial killer Ted Bundy.

About the time pubgoers were lifting a glass to her majesty in downtown Orlando, English settlers founded the town of Windermere in west Orange County. Around 1885, the Reverend Joseph Hill Scott, an Englishman, bought about 150 acres on the shore of Lake Butler. His son, Oxford graduate Dr. Stanley Scott, homesteaded the property and "bestowed the name Windermere, many believe after the famous Lake Windermere in England," west Orange historian Carl Patterson writes ("mere" means "lake," from the same root as "marine"). Soon railroad tracks linked Windermere to Kissimmee by 1889, the same year the town's plat was officially recorded. Windermere didn't really take off until 1910, though, when two men from Wauseon, Ohio, visited and knew they had found something special in its lake-strewn scenery. The pair, Dr. J.H. Johnson and J.Calvin Palmer, called Cal, bought all the land in the old town and some acreage outside and formed the Windermere Improvement Company. Years later a fashionable address for sports luminaries including golf champ Tiger Woods, the town was incorporated in 1925.

Not far from the English roots of Windermere, German settlers were making their mark about 9 miles west of downtown Orlando. Henry A. Hempel arrived from Buffalo, New York, in the 1880s and in 1885 filed a plat for the town he called Gotha, after his old-country hometown. The son of a weaver, Hempel had trained as a printer and emigrated first to England and then to the United States in 1866, where he became the foreman of a large printing press in Buffalo. When he devised a handy invention, Hempel also found the way to a new life in Florida.

An 1890s broadside promoting Orange County proclaimed that Hempel was "known all over the world as the inventor of that boon to printers, Hempel's adjustable quoin"—an expandable device used to secure metal type in a form. He was also a leading citizen of "the prosperous settlement of thrifty Germans in West Orange," the broadside said. Another early description of the town names the German-American poet Frank Siller as another

Gotha founder and also lists among the residents a "former merchant from north Germany, a famous German Prussian general, a Bavarian farmer and two German pastors' sons." These settlers had "rooted out the jungle and planted orange groves or settled down because of the wonderful climate for their health."

The house of one settler, Karl Keller, sat on pilings, and he climbed a narrow ladder to the only room, where the walls were decorated with poetry. His donkey lived under the house. Soon Keller was joined by a cousin. The men worked hard in gardens and groves during the day, nourished by dinners of fish, venison, and sweet potatoes. Both cousins had musical talents, and in the evening the songs of Franz Schubert and Robert Schumann floated on the scent of orange blossoms in the soft night air. On a Sunday afternoon in Gotha at the close of the nineteenth century, one might hear hard-working people singing in German or reading poetry as they sipped beer in their Florida paradise. No tennis courts or polo for them.

Along with English gents and German farmer-poets, the Cracker cowboys remained part of the interesting mix that peopled the Orlando area in its "phenomenal" boom. The most famous Florida cowboy, if not the most typical, was Morgan Bonaparte "Bone" Mizell, a first cousin of David Mizell, the Orange County sheriff who had been ambushed and killed in 1870. Artist Frederic Remington used Bone as the model for his painting "A Cracker Cowboy," an 1895 illustration for *Harper's* magazine that later joined the collection of the 21 Club in New York City.

Bone Mizell spent most of his time farther south in the state than Orlando, near Arcadia, but it's a safe bet tales of his exploits were told in Central Florida, where other cousins continued to live. "Kentucky had her Daniel Boone, Tennessee had her Davy Crockett, but Florida had her champion, 'Bone' Mizell, the pioneer cowboy humorist," Jim Bob Tinsley writes in his book *Florida Cow Hunter*. Ol' Bone's escapades make Davy and Daniel seem pretty gentrified, and more than a few involve whiskey—like the time Bone passed out in an Arcadia bar and woke up to find himself in a casket, resting above ground in a cemetery where his buddies had carried his boxed-up body for a joke. While the pranksters peeked from behind palmettos, Bone supposedly awoke, jumped up and hollered, "My God! It's Resurrection day, and I'm the first one up!"

The exploits of settlers such as A.M. Nicholson, a taxidermist and animal dealer, also offer reminders that Orlando in the 1880s and 1890s retained a wild edge. After arriving in 1885, Nicholson initially had a curio shop downtown, on West Church Street about a block from Orange Avenue. In the back he kept both alligators and snakes in a large pen, until one night a gator made a break for freedom, also liberating his reptilian comrades. The next morning workers at Mathews' livery barn nearby found the reptiles loose in their stable and summoned police. Nicholson was ordered to round up his critters and also remove his shop from the city's business district. He transferred his scaly enterprise home to 608 Division Street (now Division Avenue), then in the country.

Nicholson once got an order for 100 snakes from a traveling show. On the hunt to fill it, he would pick up the nonpoisonous fellows, roll them up, and pop them in the pockets of his hunting jacket. Rattlesnakes were another matter; Nicholson would gather those in double-thick cloth sack, too heavy for the snakes to chomp through. If he saw a rattler in the open, crawling from one palmetto to the other, he would get in front of it and dangle a handkerchief. While the hankie-waving had the rattler's attention, he would reach around with his other hand and pick it by the neck, and "into the sack it went," E.H. Gore wrote in his history of Orlando. In handling hundreds of snakes, Nicholson was bitten by a rattler only once, Gore says. "He treated it at once, and although his hand and arm swelled nearly to the elbow, it healed in a few days with no bad after effects."

Another entrepreneur in a less risky business changed the customs of Central Florida life and death drastically. Elijah Hand, who hailed from Indiana, was Orlando's first embalmer. Before his arrival in 1885, anyone who died in the morning was buried the same day, in the afternoon. Folks who died at night were buried the next morning. To get the word around, notices of deaths were printed on black-bordered cards and placed on store counters. After Hand set up shop, it was possible to delay funerals for several days, leaving time to notify distant friends and relatives.

Hand soon formed a partnership with E.A. Richards, Orlando's first undertaker, and in 1890, began an enterprise that combined funerals with a furniture business and livery stable. The furniture-mortuary combination wasn't unusual for the times: Cabinetmaking skills were needed to build both furniture and coffins. In 1907 Carey Hand, Elijah's son and also a trained embalmer, moved to Orlando and in 1914 bought out his father's share of the undertaking side of the business. In 1918, Carey Hand began construction of what would become Central Florida's most modern funeral home, across Pine Street from his father's two-story brick building and also across from the Grand movie palace. Carey Hand's new establishment, which opened in 1920, was the first funeral home in Florida to have its own chapel; in 1925 it added the first crematory to be built south of Cincinnati and Washington, D.C.

The records of the Carey Hand Funeral Home for Orlando's early years are in the Special Collections Department of the University of Central Florida Library and offer valuable information about the life and times of early Orlandoans, historian Pat Birkhead has noted. Some of the records are memorable. An entry for Abraham Hall, June 24, 1894, gives his age as 48, with the cause of death "heart trouble—fell dead while preaching." Besides its archives, the Hand family also left the city two of its oldest downtown buildings: The Renaissance-revival Carey Hand building at 36 West Pine Street, which now houses the university's downtown center, and the Elijah Hand building at 15 and 17 West Pine.

A few blocks west of the Hand buildings in downtown Orlando, the neighborhood that became the heart of Orlando's black community was taking shape in the 1880s and 1890s. West of Orange Avenue, what are now Parramore, Terry, West Church, and South Streets became the rough boundaries of the area, LeRoy Argrett Jr. writes in his *History of the Black Community of Orlando, Florida.*

Another black community, Jonestown, also thrived in these years east of Orange Avenue. It was first called Burnett Town, after a family of former slaves who came to Central Florida from Tallahassee in the 1880s. Not long after, white Orlando businessman James Magruder built houses in the area to sell to black residents, and the settlement became known as Jonestown after early settlers Sam and Penney Jones.

The boundaries of Jonestown, roughly, were Brown Avenue on the west and Bumby Avenue on the east. The northern edge was East Jackson Street; the south, Anderson Street. That's near where the present-day East-West Expressway cuts through Orlando by Greenwood Cemetery. Flooding was a perpetual problem in the area, and in the summer of 1904, the skies poured rain on Orlando, covering Jonestown to the tin roofs of its one-story houses.

The floods were one reason for the community's demise, but segregation was another. In 1939, a delegation of white property owners in the vicinity of East South Street went before the city commission, "to protest the rebuilding of a Negro house" that had burned in Jonestown, Bacon's history of Orlando says. "The protesters claimed a city agreement had guaranteed white occupancy in the area." In 1941, city officials declared Jonestown a slum and had it demolished. Homeowners received small sums of money, but most could not afford to buy homes elsewhere. They were moved to Griffin Park, a public housing project on the west side of town.

In the 1880s, one of the first developments in the west-side black neighborhood was built around West Central Avenue because "it was too far to walk from Jonestown to West Central for servants," Argrett writes in his history of the community. "From this beginning grew what became the Negro Section, with its homes, stores, churches and schools. . . . By 1890, the black community of west Orlando was well on its way to becoming the permanent black community of the city."

By 1890, too, Orlando's leaders turned their attention to beautifying their Phenomenal City, with an eye toward future generations who would benefit from the shade and charm of tree-lined streets. Some of Orlando's traditional oak canopy dates from a tree-planting campaign begun in 1889, when A.G. Branham & Company was awarded a contract for 400 trees to start the project. Residents also planted trees in front of their properties at their own expense. C.H. Hoffner, who lived on Lake Conway, offered to bring in oak trees and set them out and guaranteed them to live, for 50¢ each.

Other great oaks had volunteered long ago to join the landscape, sprouting where an acorn dropped or wandered. An early landmark, the Council Oak, had succumbed to one of the area's frequent lightning storms in the 1880s, but other old trees hung on, including the Southern live oak at Orlando's cozy Big Tree Park at 930 North Thornton Avenue. Because live oaks grow out instead of up, they don't reach the spectacular heights of a cypress or of redwoods in the West. Big Tree's girth of 24 feet indicates it sprouted from an acorn in about 1500, according to a sign at the park. In early Orlando, it was a favorite site for picnics and Sunday outings.

Inspired by trees like the Thornton Street oak, Orlandoans planted oaks for the future, but by the 1890s, they also felt it was time to plant a bigger monument: a courthouse worthy of the city's growth and emerging status. In 1891, the last wooden courthouse, completed in 1875 with the $10,000 loan from Jacob Summerlin, was sold to Judge J.L. Bryant, who resold it to Captain James W. Wilmott. Wilmott moved the building to East Church and Main, where it lasted until 1956 as part of a city fixture, the Tremont Hotel.

Where the Summerlin courthouse had stood, Orange County built its first important public structure, a grand new courthouse that "stood as one of the defining characteristics of downtown Orlando until it was torn down in 1957," as the engraved stone at Orlando's Heritage Square says. The cornerstone was laid on January 15, 1892, a day of great celebration. Schools were dismissed, and children were marched in orderly rows to see the ceremony. Just before the sealed box that was to be placed in the cornerstone was closed, eight-year-old Ada Bumby dropped in a penny, and the superintendent of schools, J.T. Beeks, added a document addressed to "a friend of some future age."

ORLANDO

As the city marched toward a new century, the red-brick courthouse with the 80-foot clock tower dominated Orlando's skyline. It wasn't universally beloved in the beginning. Some residents considered its turret-topped bell tower, stained-glass windows, and illuminated clock extravagances beyond the reach of the small town. The critics wondered "What in the world would little Orlando and Orange County do with such a tremendous building?" Jean Yothers, then curator of the Orange County Historical Museum, told a reporter in 1986. (Yothers's mother was Ada Bumby Yothers, in 1892 the little girl who dropped the penny in the building's cornerstone.) With time, though, the Victorian beauty became a beloved landmark. Children learned to count by hearing its bell toll the hour. No longer a lonely giant on a rustic landscape, it was joined by other sizable buildings sprouting around it.

In 1927, the building gave up its role as courthouse to the newly built neoclassic replacement that remains on Heritage Square as the home of the Orange County Regional History Center. But the 1892 structure still stood and housed offices until the mid-1950s, when county officials decided to demolish it. At the time, Americans generally tended to be enamored of all that was considered new and modern. The red Victorian clock tower was replaced by a boxy courthouse annex, since torn down, that looked a little like something from Miami Beach gone astray. It's likely that if the 1892 building had survived a few decades later, Orlandoans might have gone to great lengths to keep it. "When that courthouse was gone, I felt a real personal sense of loss," former county supervisor of elections Dixie Barber said in 1986. Orlandoans were buoyed by a sense of pride and possibility, though, when the red courthouse debuted in 1892, and they were blissfully unaware of the disaster coming at them, one that was literally chilling.

The city that boosters had crowed was built on the peel of an orange could slip on the same peel, too. It not only slipped but crashed during the one-two punch called the Great Freeze or the Big Freeze in Central Florida history. The twin freezes hit in December 1894 and February 1895. They were not the coldest weather snaps on record, agricultural historian Henry Swanson writes. But because they touched the lives of so many people and reduced the citrus industry to almost zero, they are remembered as the most damaging of all the major freezes—at least until almost 100 years later, when killer cold returned in the 1980s to again devastate the citrus industry in Orange County.

In the 1894–1895 debacle, the first freeze hit on December 29, Swanson writes, but warm weather and rain returned in January. The sap began to flow in the shocked trees, which also pushed out new growth. When the second freeze struck on February 7, 1895, with 18-degree temperatures, the trees literally popped like pistol shots as the freezing sap burst open the bark. As a result, the growers lost both their crop and their trees, many of which were killed to the ground.

The first freeze, the one in December, was bad even by itself, without the February follow-up. A memoir by Karl Abbott, whose parents were running the San Juan Hotel on Orlando's main street, Orange Avenue, painted a vivid picture of the hotel lobby in an uproar as the big thermometers in front of the hotel indicated unusual cold. Abbott wrote:

> About nine that night, a fine looking gray-haired man in a black frock coat and Stetson hat walked up the street in front of the hotel and looked at the thermometer, groaned 'Oh, my God!,' and shot himself through the head. For

three days the icy winds blew over a dead world. The gloom in the San Juan was something you could touch and feel.

Of eight banks in the county, only the First National Bank of Sanford survived.

The Great Freeze hit the English colony hard. None of the ads and brochures the gentleman growers had read back home mentioned the possibility of financial devastation by weather. Although some of the English growers weathered the crisis, others fled, and quickly. One account says some departed so fast they left "tables set and dishes unwashed."

Despite the devastation and later freezes that followed in the 1890s, Central Florida's citrus industry would recover, as would Orlando, and the city of about 2,400 souls soldiered on toward the new century. Life went on. In 1899, the city council decided it was time to number the houses in town, and J.M. Slemons delighted the younger generation by building a "shute-the-shute"—a slide—at Lake Eola. In 1900, the first newspaper devoted to news of the black community was started in Orlando, when G.C. Henderson began publication of the *Florida Christian Recorder*, a weekly that continued for 15 years.

As the century closed, Orlando's police force boasted three officers: Charles Maltbie, W.J. Pope, and Charles "Slewfoot" Carter. The story goes that Carter kept a vinegar barrel behind the city jail downtown on Oak Street (now Wall Street). After he once caught several boys stealing, he punished them by putting them over the barrel while they got 25 lashes with a heavy strap. Supposedly none of the miscreants ran afoul of "Slewfoot" Carter again.

Not far from Carter's vinegar barrel was the large Webber home at 111 North Orange Avenue that Braxton Beacham bought in 1900. (In 1907, he would be elected mayor of Orlando.) Beacham had made a bunch of green money growing celery in Sanford, and he would spend the staggering sum of $75,000 transforming the house into Orlando's showplace. He later bought the old county jail, tore it down, and built the Beacham Theater on Orange Avenue. It opened in late 1921 and for many years reigned as Orlando's leading movie palace.

A great Central Florida institution also got its start in 1900, when Dr. R.L. Harris bought an old farmhouse on Lake Estelle, plus 52 acres on the west and north sides of the lake. Harris added several cottages and transformed the house into a tuberculosis sanitarium, where he treated patients with fresh air and good food as well as medicines, creating the nucleus of what would become Florida Hospital. Harris also has been credited with owning the first motor car in Orlando, although several other daring souls were close behind him.

Whether in autos or yet on horseback, Orlandoans forged into the twentieth century. Sure, some folks had fled, but plenty stayed. The Phenomenal City had been tested. Cattle feuds, a blazing fire, and killer freezes had come and gone, but Orlando, nestled around its big red clock tower, wasn't going anywhere. It harbored too many dreams for the future.

Chapter Five

BRIGHT AND DARK DAYS
IN THE CITY BEAUTIFUL

Settling into the 1900s, Orlandoans decided it was time for a fresh image. Perhaps "The Phenomenal City" seemed a little old-fashioned, and although Orange County continued to grow, the boom days before the Great Freeze were a memory. Such heady times of growth would come again, but not for a couple of decades, after a war on a scale no one yet imagined—the war to end all wars, Americans believed. Embracing new inventions from movies to motor cars, Orlando became more sophisticated, and it sought a motto to match.

A fresh movement to dress up the city with palms, azaleas, and flowering shrubs inspired the hunt for a new name, too. In a 1908 contest, a number of candidates were submitted, including "The Queen City," "The Magic City," "The Picturesque City," and "The Health City." But Orlandoans thought Mrs. W.S. Branch Sr. got it just right with her winning entry: "The City Beautiful." Who wouldn't want to come to such a pleasant-sounding place? As it turned out, a rather amazing variety of folks did.

One of them, Helen Gardner, came to Orlando and then went on to become about as big a star as early silent pictures boasted. She arrived in the city about 1902, shortly after her marriage that year to Duncan Clarkston Pell of the socially prominent Pells of New York and Rhode Island. Pell had begun to winter in Central Florida with his first wife, Anna, in the mid-1890s; his uncle was Leslie Pell-Clarke, the bicycle-riding gent beloved by the English colony for his hospitality.

In 1901, Duncan Pell began a messy divorce that made a splash in *The New York Times*. That same year he also bought part of the old Mizell homestead on Lake Rowena; David Mizell, the Reconstruction sheriff slain in 1870 during the cattle-range wars, is buried nearby (the home is now the Leu House at Orlando's Harry P. Leu Gardens).

Pell transformed the Mizell farmhouse into a comfortable country home, suitable for a gentleman citrus grower. In 1902, within a week of his Florida divorce, he married Helen Gardner of Binghamton, New York, in a Connecticut ceremony. He was 33; she had just turned 18. In Orlando, the Pells circulated in the polo and party set. On weekends, they entertained at the Lake Rowena house; during the week they lived downtown at the elegant Wyoming Hotel.

Young Mrs. Pell turned heads. "All the men would watch her walk down Orange Avenue with her hourglass figure," Orlando native Lillian Lindorf remembered many years later. Before too long, Helen Gardner walked away from Pell and Orlando for good. In 1906, he put the house on Lake Rowena up for sale. The role of a society wife, it seems, was not for the young beauty. The movie business was then based in New York City, and roles such as Cleopatra were waiting.

Between 1911 and 1930, Gardner appeared in 22 movies, ranging from *Vanity Fair* (1911) to *A Princess of Baghdad* (1913) to *Monte Carlo* (1930). In 1912, when she was 28, she founded her own production company, Helen Gardner Players. It was a remarkable step for a woman in a business run by men, says Julie Cole, co-author of the book *Orlando's Leu House*, which chronicles the history of the home on Lake Rowena and its occupants.

Silent-screen vamp Theda Bara became better known in film history as a curvy, kohl-eyed siren, but Cole makes a convincing case that Bara based her style on Gardner, particularly in the six-reel epic, *Helen Gardner in Cleopatra* (1912). Billed as "the most beautiful motion picture ever made," Gardner's version was the first Queen of the Nile to be put on film. Like many other silent stars, she did not make the transition to talking pictures; her fame was at its peak from 1912 to 1915. In the early 1950s, she returned to live her last years in Orlando, where she died on November 20, 1968, at 84.

About the time the future Cleopatra had first made a splash in town, another new Orlando-area resident arrived who would also gain a national reputation, but in horticulture rather than cinema. Born in rural Wisconsin in 1853, a year after his parents emigrated from Germany, Henry Nehrling bought his stake in the sunshine sight unseen. Looking for a place to pursue his interest in tropical plants, in 1884 he purchased a 40-acre farm after hearing about the nearby village of Gotha and its population of German farmer-intellectuals. He first saw his land in 1886 and then made lengthy visits every year or two, until he and his family were able to make a permanent move from Milwaukee 20 years after his initial purchase.

In 1902, Nehrling bought the 1880 house he named Palm Cottage and had it moved by wagon in sections onto his land, where he surrounded it with plants from all over the world. After a trip to Palm Cottage and its gardens years later, the pre-eminent Florida horticulturist David Fairchild called it "one of the most interesting places in all of Florida." Nehrling, Fairchild said, "was a mine of information regarding plants. . . . He is a real pioneer and student of nature of the old-fashioned kind."

During a visit to the Brazilian exhibit at the World's Columbian Exposition in Chicago in 1893, Nehrling had become fascinated with the caladium, which, thanks to him, would become a fixture of Florida landscaping. The color and delicacy of the plants made an impression on Nehrling he never forgot. Once settled in Gotha, he began experimenting in earnest and in one year grew as many as 250,000 caladium plants, including about 1,500 named varieties.

Eventually, Nehrling created Florida's first experimental botanical garden, where he tested more than 3,000 new and rare plants for the U.S. Department of Agriculture—plants that became the foundation for Florida's thriving nursery industry. Nehrling died in 1929; he is buried not far from his Gotha home, at Woodlawn Cemetery.

Like Gardner and Nehrling, Mary Augusta Safford exemplifies the range of folks who were drawn to the Orlando area in the early twentieth century. In 1911, when she was 60, Safford exchanged her Unitarian pastorate in Des Moines, Iowa, for the life of an orange grower and women's rights activist in Orlando. Like Henry Nehrling, she bought her piece of Florida by long distance, without laying her eyes on it. Her reputation as compelling orator followed her to Orlando. In 1917, shortly after President Wilson declared war on Germany, residents packed the Lucerne Theatre to hear Safford's featured address at a patriotic rally; she was the only woman on the program.

Safford had begun speaking in public as a child in Illinois. The story goes that she practiced delivering sermons from a tree-stump pulpit on her family's farm in Hamilton, near the mighty Mississippi. Women were expected to do their church work in the kitchen and their praying in the pews, but young Mary had other plans. She became a Unitarian minister by the time she was 28—the central figure in a group of clergywomen who dominated their church's development on the frontier for the rest of the century. Her friend Eleanor Gordon, who grew up on a neighboring farm, also became a Unitarian minister. Many years after their Great Plains girlhood, in 1912 Gordon would move to Orlando like her old friend and become the organizing minister of the city's First Unitarian Church.

Both Safford and Gordon came to Orlando through friendships forged in Iowa. In 1905, Safford officiated at the St. Louis marriage of venerable Orlandoan Mahlon Gore, then in his 60s, and Caroline Groninger, who had known Safford in Sioux City years before. Gore, who moved from Iowa to Orlando in 1880, was the newspaper man who had managed to get out a fire edition in 1884, when the city's business district went up in flames. Later, he served as mayor in the 1890s.

After buying an orange grove on Mahlon Gore's advice, Safford visited the Gores in Orlando and, in 1911, returned to stay. Her Illinois-farm childhood came in handy in her Florida retirement. Unlike some of the English colonists in the 1880s, she often pruned and cultivated the trees herself at her grove near Lake Conway. She also cultivated the cause of women's rights. In 1913, Safford organized the Florida Equal Suffrage Group in Orlando, and the following year she helped organize the Men's Equal Suffrage League, led by Mayor E.F. Sperry, a fellow Unitarian. Her efforts paid off. In March 1919, Orlando women gained the right to vote in all municipal elections, more than a year before the national woman suffrage amendment was ratified.

When Safford died in 1927, she left a message to comfort grieving friends that was typically forward-looking: "I am eager to find out what lies beyond the limit of our seeing and of our hearing and do not think the Over There will be any the less interesting than the here, since the universe seems to be of one piece, offering boundless possibilities of growth."

It wasn't spiritual growth, though, but growing stacks of tourist dollars that some Orlandoans had on their minds, and the city's boosters trumpeted its charms with increasing fervor. Central Floridians had started wooing visitors early in the years B.D.—"Before Disney" in Orlando-speak. The chamber of commerce had been organized as the Board of Trade in 1886. And, in contrast to the pioneer years when some forthright soul had slapped the name Mosquito County on a big chunk of Florida, early Orlando promoters had almost from the start freely embellished the facts, especially when it came to bugs. In Orlando, one would find "freedom from troublesome insects," a cheery promotional 1910 booklet proclaimed.

Other attractions included "the best drinking water on earth." The city's shaded streets nestled below "the Southern sky, aglow with the kindling tints of a tropical clime." Here the writer climbed to new heights of hyperbole: "Many who come to Orlando for relief from the cold learn to like the summer climate even better than they do the winter," the little book declared, in a statement few who have lived through a Florida August would embrace. But Orlando wasn't just Florida; it was the City Beautiful. The booklet urged folks to come and see for themselves:

Bright and Dark Days in the City Beautiful

> Frequenters of other sections [of the state], who have found their chief troubles
> to be clouds of mosquitoes and myriads of gnats and fleas, should visit Orlando.
> Nearly all our people sleep without canopies over their beds, and that is a sure sign
> of freedom from mosquitoes.

Truth-telling or the lack of it in promoting the Orlando area produced one of the best true tales from the city's early days. The story is linked to one of only two mausoleums in Orlando's city-owned Greenwood Cemetery, begun in the 1880s. Karl Abbott told the story in his book *Open for the Season*, about memories of the San Juan Hotel.

A young Abbott was with one of the Englishmen who lived at the hotel, Fred Weeks, in 1910 one day when Weeks was out scouting the countryside in a mule-drawn buckboard. They drove by a 20-acre tract that was being developed. "We couldn't see the back half because so many brush fires were going and the smoke was thick," Abbott wrote. The three owners "extolled the fertility of the soil and the beauty of the location," and Weeks bought the land. When he returned the next day and discovered the back acres were useless swamp, he got mad and then he got even.

Weeks bought a lot near the cemetery entrance and placed on it a large tombstone carved with the scoundrels' names and a biblical inscription from the book of Luke: "There was a man come down from Jericho and fell among thieves." Prodded by the guffaws that swept Orlando, the three real-estate developers gave Weeks his money back and also bought the cemetery plot from him and took down the stone. But Weeks couldn't let go of his vendetta. He built an impressive mausoleum at Greenwood and on the door repeated the quotation. Some accounts say he also repeated the names, which have since been obliterated. When Weeks died in 1918, he was buried in the tomb. Mrs. Weeks was having none of it, though; she hadn't cared for her husband's revenge tactics. When she died, her remains were taken back to her former home in Indiana. At Greenwood, the "thieves" inscription remains clearly legible on the Weeks tomb.

The year Weeks, an Englishman, was fuming over his swampy purchase, Orlando gained another lasting tradition with a British connection. According to E.H. Gore's *History of Orlando* (1949), Charles Lord brought the first two pairs of swans to Orlando from England in 1910. A prominent Orlando businessman who had arrived from England himself in 1885 with the influx of his countrymen, Lord remembered the swans he had seen on the Thames River in his youth. On a visit back to England, he bought four of them, a white pair and a black pair. He sent the birds by an express service to Orlando for the princely sum of $95, for which the city reimbursed him. The swans arrived in November 1910, and Lord installed them on what was called the Hughey peninsula near his Lake Lucerne home. They were cared for by city employees. It wasn't long before there was trouble at the halcyon scene. Some of the swans had to be moved to Lake Eola for their safety. It seems that one of the male birds Lord had imported was a doozy, the Terminator in formidable feathered form.

Visitors can still examine this specimen for themselves. Billy the Swan, a.k.a. the "Tyrant of Lake Lucerne" or "Billy Bluebeard," survives as a masterly work of taxidermy in a glass case at the Orange County Regional History Center, just a few blocks from Lake Eola. He's a fine specimen a young cygnet might well model itself after. Gore's history of Orlando claims

ORLANDO

Billy was 75 when he died of old age, in the early 1930s. Another source says he only made it to 55. In any case, that's far longer than the swans at Orlando's Lake Eola Park seem to live these days, with all of the hazards of urban life.

Perhaps they need some of Billy's fire. During mating and nesting season especially, he not only terrorized children on their way to Delaney School, but he also chased cars. And there's blood on his bill, metaphorically speaking. His nickname "Billy Bluebeard" comes from the enduring story that Billy drowned his original mate, Sally, because she neglected the nest or had eyes for another. "When Sally, Billy's mate, was murdered, her lovely white body was laid to rest in a grave dug under one of the large oak trees" by Lake Lucerne, Gore's history says. Clearly, Orlando is a town that takes its swans seriously.

When Billy's time came to meet his maker, Charlie Morgan, manager of the Swan & Company Dry Goods Store on West Church Street, asked for the body, which he took it to a taxidermist. The bird was on display in a glass case at the store for a number of years until he was placed in a the county's museum at the top of the old red-brick county courthouse in the 1940s. Both the swan and his wood-and-glass case were given a proper renovation.

About the time Billy began his reign over Lake Lucerne, Central Florida boosters turned their thoughts to putting together an exposition to promote the area. In 1886, the city built a frame exposition hall on the shores of Lake Eola, where the Rosalind Club now sits, and threw a party, a county fair of sorts, to show off agricultural gems and to enjoy horse racing and other amusements. Lake Eola was so full after a rainy season that folks entering the hall had to walk across boards or get their feet wet.

It had been a good time, but like so much else, the fair fell victim to the killer freezes of 1894 and 1895. By 1909 or so, though, the City Beautiful was in shape again to show off and have a good time. Led by W.R. O'Neal, H.H. Dickson, Harry Beeman, C.H. Hoffner, and others, residents formed the Orange County Fair Association and put up several exhibit buildings, barns, and stock pens at what would become the fairgrounds on West Livingston Street.

With the promotional zeal that runs deep in Orlando's roots, the fair association put on a parade of flower-bedecked automobiles, but its members had something far more spectacular in mind. Orlandoans would see a man fly. They offered a whopping $1,500 to the first aviator who could stay in the air for five minutes at one time, flying over the new exhibition grounds. (The traditional version is that the flying contest happened in 1910, but recent research suggests it may have been in early 1911.)

Three contestants hoped to win the $1,500, but only one had the right stuff: pioneering aviator Lincoln Beachey of California, the 27th person to be licensed as a pilot in the United States and a dashing figure in his biplane built by the Wrights. Called "the man without nerves," Beachey went on to thrill crowds across America; his Orlando triumph was one of his early exploits. In August 1911, he set a world altitude record of 11,150 feet in Chicago by climbing until his plane ran out of gas and gliding back to earth. Also that year, he flew in Tampa at night over the city, only a year after the first recorded night flight, in Knoxville, Tennessee. But on March 14, 1915, less than two weeks after his 28th birthday, Beachey's luck ran out. During an exhibition flight at the Panama-Pacific International Exposition in San Francisco, his short, spectacular life ended when he crashed into the cold water near the Golden Gate.

goodwill that in their minds permeated the area's history. Black people, on the other hand, recount a legacy of fear that would cause children years later to scramble down on the floors of cars to hide if they had to drive through Ocoee on the way to a school event. Even among whites, it's not uncommon to hear stories about black delivery drivers who would go out of their way to avoid passage through Ocoee in the 1950s and 1960s. Both races have borne the scars of November 2, 1920 and the days following.

Many details of story remain elusive. On election day, at least two black men, July Perry and Mose Norman, tried to vote in the west Orange agricultural community of Ocoee, where Perry was a powerful landowner and labor contractor. By the bloody night's end, Norman had vanished. At least eight people were dead, two white men and at least six black people, including Perry, who was lynched. His body was cut down from a tree the next day in Orlando. His death and the other fatalities represented only part of the riot's legacy.

During a 10-hour rampage, a white mob stormed into Ocoee and burned churches and homes. On election night and in the days following, the entire black population, at least 200 people, fled. What had been a racially mixed town became an all-white community for decades. Before the riot, about half of Ocoee's residents were black, according to research by Ocoee historian Lester Dabbs. The only known survivor in 2001, the late Armstrong Hightower, who was 13 in 1920, told an interviewer that he and his sister hid in a tree as their world turned to flames. It was his sister's birthday and they had been preparing for a party. "I lost my childhood," he replied to a question about reparations. "What you think they oughtn' to pay me for that?"

"No one really knows how many died," says Francina Boykin, one of the key researchers into the event. "They left everything behind, fled with only the clothes on their backs." A subsequent investigation by the National Association for the Advancement of Colored People put the death toll at as many as 50.

In a 2002 interview, Mildred Board, then 88, remembered the night vividly, including the flight of black Ocoee residents into Apopka. "You could see the smoke from about eight or nine miles away," she said. "How did you get here?" her father asked one man who appeared in his nightshirt. "I ran like a rabbit in the wind," the man said. Board also remembered the Perrys, friends of her family's. "They were lovely people," she said. Children liked to visit the Perry home because July Perry always had candy for them.

A 50-year-old church deacon, Perry has played a different role in the varying accounts of the tragedy. To some whites, he was possibly a killer, responsible for the deaths of two white men who had come in a posse to his house. To others, he was a hero, immortalized by writer and folklorist Zora Neale Hurston, the Orlando area's most famous daughter. "So night dusted down on Ocoee, with mobs seeking blood and ashes and July Perry standing his lone watch over his rights to life and property," Hurston wrote in an essay in the 1930s.

Perry and Norman were prosperous, powerful men for their times. Each owned a grove, farmland, and a home. Perry owned a truck; Norman, a car. And between them, Norman and Perry controlled the labor market for black farm workers in the Ocoee area. Efforts by these men to vote—and, likely, to encourage others to vote—would have put them at odds with a system of laws designed to disenfranchise black people across the South in a backlash to Reconstruction.

ORLANDO

One-party rule ensured that the Democratic primary decided most elections; African Americans were told "white voters only." In Florida, the major parties played reverse roles from their later associations with civil rights. Republicans were the liberals, at least in terms of voting rights, but they had only a token political presence in Florida. The GOP did have at least one figure of influence in Orange County: Judge John M. Cheney, owner of the Orlando Water and Light Company. In 1920, he was the Republican candidate for U.S. senator.

In the weeks before election day, rumors circulated that Cheney and another influential Orlandoan, W.R. O'Neal, had been meeting with African Americans in Ocoee to encourage them to vote. In a November 6 letter to an Ohio senator, Republican state campaign chief Alexander Akerman, an associate of Cheney's, made clear the party had aimed at all voters, "entirely ignoring the race question." Democrats had "immediately set up a howl that the election of a Republican president meant Negro domination, black heels on white necks," Akerman wrote. Sometimes the howl became a chilling whisper. A few weeks before the election, a letter from the Florida grand master of the Ku Klux Klan warned Cheney and O'Neal what would happen if they persisted in encouraging blacks to vote on election day: "And now if you are a scholar, you know that history repeats itself, and that he who resorts to your kind of game is handling edged tools," the letter concluded. "We shall always enjoy White Supremacy in this country, and he who interferes must face the consequences."

The Saturday night before election day in 1920, the KKK marched through Orlando streets "500 strong," the Sunday newspaper reported, characterizing the performance as "a revival of that great secret organization which guarded the honor of the South in the troubled days" after the Civil War. The so-called invisible empire had a much higher profile than it would in later years in America, after deaths such as July Perry's sparked resignations and government investigations. But in the early 1920s, it was not uncommon for Klansmen to parade in daylight at Florida civic events, such as a 1922 "Tourist's Day" celebration in Brooksville recorded in a photo in the state archives. Eleanor Fisher, a granddaughter of Orlando pioneer Joseph Bumby, can remember as a child seeing the hooded marchers pass down Orlando's Orange Avenue some years after the 1920 march, a ghostly, silent column of intimidation.

For years, the location of Perry's grave was a mystery. In 1998, Curtis Michelson and Francina Boykin of Democracy Forum, a group dedicated to shedding light on the event, discovered Perry's death certificate in state records and learned his grave was at Orlando's Greenwood Cemetery. Investigating cemetery records, Democracy Forum members learned the location of the unmarked grave, where they continued their tradition of memorial vigils on the anniversary of the Ocoee Riot.

Since the late 1990s, the efforts of Democracy Forum and another grass-roots group, the Ocoee-based West Orange Reconciliation Task Force, have brought the story of the Ocoee Riot from the shadows of the past. A play about the event, *The Whirlwind Passeth* by Bernadette Adams Davis and Kevin Meehan, and a short documentary film, *Ocoee: Legacy of the Election Day Massacre*, have helped bring public awareness to the event and its aftermath.

The filmmakers, Sandra Krasa and Bianca White, focused especially on two descendants of men who had key roles in the story. Growing up in Ocoee, James Fleming, a grandson of Colonel Sam Salisbury, had heard his grandfather's memories of the election night when Salisbury was wounded after he was asked to lead a posse to July Perry's home. Salisbury, a young man in 1920, had briefly been police chief of Orlando. The other descendant, the Reverend Stephen Nunn, as a boy had also heard from his grandmother, Coretha Perry Caldwell, about what transpired at the Perry house that night. July Perry was a grandfather he never knew.

In talking about their family memories, Fleming and Nunn were breaking the silence with which Central Floridians, both black and white, long treated the memory of Ocoee. Such a silence has been a common American response to race riots, says the Reverend Jerry Girley, a founder of the West Orange Reconciliation Task Force. The idea is "let sleeping dogs lie." What's the point in digging up a painful past, people ask. Girley is ready with a response. When you visit a doctor for the first time, you don't just start with a physical exam, he says. You answer a clipboard full of questions; you give your medical history. That's because there's a predictive value in knowing your history. There's a path to greater understanding.

Along that path, the West Orange Reconciliation Task Force placed a stone memorial on July Perry's long-unmarked grave on the 82nd anniversary of the Ocoee Riot. The Reverend Nunn, Perry's grandson, traveled from Tampa to speak at the ceremony.

"The sleeping giant from yesterday of Ocoee has awakened," Nunn said in cadences greeted by "amens" from the crowd. "He has declared that there are giant footsteps for democracy today, and they're being imprinted upon the hearts and the minds and the souls of people everywhere." "To me, this truly marks the beginning of the healing process," Ocoee City Commissioner Nancy Parker said. "This is where we go forward."

Chapter Six

SIZZLE AND FIZZLE
IN THE ROARING TWENTIES

The wave of prosperity and good times rolling over America in the 1920s splashed down hard on Florida, inspiring a land boom that would double the city of Orlando's population in five years and triple it by 1930, to more than 27,000. During the same decade, Orange County's population more than doubled to almost 50,000 in 1930. Construction crews rushed to build churches, schools, and other public buildings to meet the needs of the surge of new residents.

In October 1925, the *Orlando Morning Sentinel* tallied the value of building permits in the city for the year at more than $5.5 million. Even in inflated boom times, that was serious money. You could buy a good dinner for a dollar and a fine pair of shoes for $5. The contract for one 1925 structure, Park Lake Presbyterian Church, was for $50,000. Of its 518 charter members, almost 60 percent were "from every part of the United States and Canada," the church's 1926 yearbook says.

Riding the railroads and the country's fledgling road system, newcomers scrambled to own a piece of sunshine, or at least get a look at what all the fuss was about. It was an interesting crowd. On a motorcycle trip with her husband, Bill, who would later found Alcoholic Anonymous, traveler Lois Wilson noted that while Orlando's many lakes "make it a charming residential city," the folks on the downtown streets were "a motley crew—sharpers, aristocrats, tough looking women, get-rich-quickies, and just plain people." "It looked like the world on wheels was coming to Florida," Orlando-born developer Carl Dann wrote as he looked back on the heady decade.

Where there's a boom, though, it's likely a bust isn't far behind. In Florida, the bubble burst well before the stock market crash of 1929. Two nightmare hurricanes in South Florida in 1926 and 1928 helped pull the flimsy foundations out from a real-estate frenzy driven in part by the lure of fast turnover and quick profits. "The phenomenon began at Miami Beach, spread through Dade County, moved up the east and west coasts and infused Central Florida," historian William Rogers writes in *The New History of Florida*. "To many Florida seemed a lotus land, and there was no shortage of individuals anxious to exploit its potential."

Dann, the founder of Orlando's Dubsdread golf course, shrewdly assessed the fizz and the fizzle in his 1929 memoir, *Carl Dann's Vicissitudes and Casathrophics*. During the Florida boom, too many folks muscled into the real estate business who had no business being there, he wrote. They were lured by a barrage of news reports that unwittingly caused things to get out of hand.

Real estate men would report their sales to the papers, often exaggerating the price.

> By and by, these articles became so numerous that the outside real estate men, and, in fact, merchants in every line of business decided that the real estate man was becoming rich, so they entered the game. They all had friends, and they sold

to them; a great many of them made money; that started the ball rolling. . . . It finally became nothing more than a gambling machine. Each man was buying on a shoe string, betting dollars that a bigger fool than he would come along and buy his option before the title company could deliver the title and final payment would have to be made.

The "gambling machine" produced a great many of what Dann called "Yes" developments. Signs along the roads leading to their sites blasted prospective buyers with assurances. "Will we have water? Yes! Will we have electric lights? Yes!" In the end, many of them never produced a street or a house, much less water and lights. The entrances to these promised Shangri-las in the swamps were usually marked by a great arch made of a hasty coat of plaster slapped over wooden lathes, Dann wrote. A few sturdier versions of this kind of grand gateway survive in Central Florida. During these years, signs everywhere touted "proposed" million dollar Venetian pools or "proposed" million dollar hotels. "Friends," Dann wrote, "you can not live in, or eat, anything proposed."

Thousands of new residents did want to live and eat in Orlando, and Dann and other hometown developers were ready for them. The story goes that one of the founders of Orlando's popular College Park neighborhood advised developing the area for the common man, "because there are so many of them." That area's bungalow-lined streets still retain the feeling of a small town just blocks from the city's downtown.

College Park got its start in 1925 when David A. Cooper, S. Howard Atha and Harry W. Barr of the Cooper-Atha-Barr Company, called Cabco, began developing near Rosemere, one of the many Orlando subdivisions pioneered by Walter Rose. Rose had begun using college-named streets in 1921: Princeton, Harvard, Yale, and Cornell, and later Vanderbilt, DePauw, and Amherst. They had the ring of class and stability.

Cabco extended the existing college-named streets to the west and added new ones. In January 1926, the company ("Phone 2400"), unveiled a section of College Park's Country Club section: 188 lots priced from $1,500 to $4,000. "College Park had its inception in a dream," the ad said. "And that dream has already become a most potent reality. It is a solid and permanent development."

Cabco's ads sought to reassure investors of the firm's sincerity and stability through a cartoon figure called Mr. Cabco. "You've got to have something a little catchy," one of the sign painters for the firm had told Cabco's owners. "Mr. Cabco has been very busy of late," a 1926 newspaper ad proclaimed. "He is paving streets, laying sidewalks, clearing and beautifying land, and building substantial homes. . . . You've known him for years—he is a friend of yours." There would be no plaster arches, no "Yes!" developments for Mr. Cabco.

Some new arrivals in the Roaring Twenties sought and bought digs that were considerably more grand than the cozy homes of College Park. In Florida, "we developed a sun-parlor and playground for the United States," Carl Dann wrote, and not all wealthy Northerners wanted to winter in Palm Beach. For many, the lakes and tree-lined streets of the Orlando area were just fine.

One of the most colorful was Grace Mather-Smith, a grande dame who landed in the charming west Orange County town of Oakland. The wife of a wealthy Northern industrialist,

Mather-Smith inspired stories of various Auntie Mame–style escapades. According to one, once she was stopped for a $10 ticket as she sped into downtown Orlando to stock up for one of her lavish parties. Undismayed, she flipped a $20 bill to the officer, quipping, "Keep the change, Buster, because I'll be coming through again on my way back."

Some of the people rolling down from the North in the 1920s didn't travel in such fast company, but they seem to have enjoyed themselves royally. Car campers called Tin Can Tourists blossomed in the early days of auto travel from the North to Florida. Sometimes they fastened empty tin cans to the hoods of their Tin Lizzies to announce themselves to kindred spirits on the road.

The Tin Canners took their name from a devotion to bring-along cuisine that irked Florida restaurateurs. "Never having been so far from their own kitchens, and unsure of what to expect in the way of provisions on the road, they loaded up with canned meat and canned vegetables and even canned fruit—they brought their own fruit to Florida," historian David Thornburg writes. The locals were amazed. Like their buddies in the food business, the hoteliers were not delighted; one of the oft-repeated quips by the Tin Canners' detractors was that they arrived from the North with one shirt and a $20 bill, and changed neither.

Despite the vogue for auto camping, hotels blossomed during the boom, and a chamber of commerce brochure touted a variety of choices for the traveler, led by the latest incarnation of the San Juan Hotel ("250 rooms, 250 baths—Orlando's largest and finest") and the new Angebilt across Orange Avenue, near the city's core intersection of Orange and Central Boulevard. Debuting in March 1923, the million-dollar Angebilt stood on the former site of the Rosalind Club, a private social club for ladies that continues to the present day, now meeting in its building by Lake Eola.

The Angebilt hotel's builder, J.F. Ange, president of the Bank of Orange, could bear witness to the volatile nature of the land business in Central Florida. In 1921, he had been shot and wounded in the back by R.D. Waring, an Orlando real estate man, at Ange's home at 13 East Amelia Avenue, according to Eve Bacon's history of Orlando. Waring was apparently upset over a real estate deal in Kissimmee. He was sentenced to six months in jail for the shooting, which did not seriously hurt Ange.

A few blocks away, at 511 West South Street, a hotel opened at the end of boom that survived the bust in robust fashion and went on to a special place in Central Florida history. In segregation days, it was hard for black travelers to find accommodations, and Dr. William Monroe Wells took action. One of Orlando's first African-American physicians and a community leader, he obtained a building permit in 1926 for a two-story brick hotel, which opened to great success in 1929.

Next to the hotel during its heyday in the 1930s and 1940s was the South Street Casino night club (later called the Quarterback Club), where some of America's top musical talents stopped to entertain as they traveled the South during segregation. Cab Calloway, Count Basie, Ella Fitzgerald, Lionel Hampton, Dinah Washington, Ray Charles, and many more musical greats played or lodged on South Street, where they found a home away from home at Wells' hotel.

The building is one of Central Florida's preservation success stories. Vacant since about 1970, it was brought to a new life in the late 1990s. Now, the doctor's hotel—originally called the Wellsbilt—is home to the Wells' Built Museum of African American History and Culture and, upstairs, to sunny offices for groups including the African American Chamber of Commerce. It's on the National Register of Historic Places.

Another historic brick hotel building survives from the late 1920s in Winter Garden, where trains delivered visitors to its front door. The Edgewater Hotel catered to a far-flung clientele of travelers. Mostly men, they arrived to do business with area citrus and produce growers or to fish the waters of Lake Apopka, the biggest freshwater lake in Florida behind giant Okeechobee. The rooftop of the three-story hotel offered a spectacular view of the great lake. At the water's edge, the hotel kept 20 rowboats and a houseboat for the pleasure of sporting enthusiasts. The large stone fireplace in the Edgewater's lobby was added in the 1930s to boost the hotel's rustic allure as a vacation destination for sportsmen of taste. Stories persist that Humphrey Bogart and Clark Gable were among the lodgers who sought relaxation at the hotel and on the lake's then-bountiful waters. (Present-day Lake Apopka is being reclaimed from decades of agricultural pollution.)

In spite of the increasing influx of visitors and snowbirds from the North, Orlando remained, more than many Florida cities, a year-round town. That was part of its appeal for folks who wanted to put down roots and become part of a community, like the Ebsen family from Illinois.

Long before the family's son, Buddy, gained a place in the pop-culture pantheon as Uncle Jed Clampett of *The Beverly Hillbillies*, he won rave reviews for his football prowess at Orlando High School. "One of the best guards OHS has ever had," yearbook editors wrote in 1926. "He was strong on both offense and defense. He had the old grit and fight that it takes to make a football player." Ebsen's dad, Christian, came from a small village on the border of Germany and Denmark; his mother, Frances, was from Latvia. They met ice skating on Lake Michigan and settled in Belleville, Illinois, a town with a large German-American population where Ebsen's dad coached basketball, offered dancing lessons, and taught what was called "physical culture"—a kind of physical education.

In 1920, when Buddy was 12, his mother's poor health inspired a family move to Florida. After a year in Palm Beach, already a seasonal town for rich folks, the Ebsens thought it wise to seek out a new hometown where people would want dance lessons all year long, not just in the winter season. Christian Ebsen "looked around and found Orlando," Buddy Ebsen later recalled. "He fell in love with it because it was a family town, a year-round town. And it was beautiful."

They first rented a home near Lake Eola and eventually settled at 9 South Hyer Avenue, where Ebsen's father built a small house and later a dance studio. Through the years, hundreds—probably thousands—of young Orlandoans took classes at The Ebsen School of Dance, and Christian Ebsen became a significant figure in the history of the arts in Central Florida. Like many newcomers over the years, the Ebsens were able to nurture their dreams in Orlando and leave a legacy for future generations.

Perhaps a young Buddy Ebsen was among the crowd at the opening of high school in 1923, when the city's growth-fueled optimism "was positively contagious," according to a news report. "The hardest cynic in Orlando, had he been present, would have been thawed down to a jolly boy, proud of life and mighty glad to walk the streets of Orlando," the paper said.

ORLANDO

Orlandoans could be proud that school enrollment had skyrocketed from 400 students and 14 teachers in 1911 to about 2,600 students as the fall term began in 1923.

The city's grade schools had registered 1,600 pupils and 41 teachers. The newspaper listed the city's grammar schools as Magnolia, Delaney, West Central, Opportunity, and Hillcrest. Delaney School, built in 1920, now houses the Beardall Senior Center and is likely Orlando's oldest surviving public school building. About 1,000 students were enrolled in high school and junior high.

Samples of the high school humor of the day survive in yearbooks such as *The Yellow Jacket*, produced by students at the Oakland-Winter Garden School, which preceded Lakeview High School in west Orange County. Student editors often added classmates' names to spice the repartee:

> Mary B: "I think the Charleston is awful."
>
> Louise J.: "I can't learn it either."
>
> Prof.: "Ever had Economics?"
>
> Howie F.: "No, just the measles and chickenpox."
>
> Joe K.: "Bob says he doesn't enjoy squeezing his girl."
>
> Bruce B.: "Probably she's a lemon."
>
> She: "I learned to smoke cigarettes in Paris."
>
> He: "Good thing you didn't go to Norway—they smoke herring there."
>
> Q: "Do you file your fingernails?"
>
> A: "No, I just throw them away after I cut them off."
>
> Q: "Oh, Doctor, what should I do for Tom's ears; they stick out so?"
>
> A: "Very simple, Madam; give him a radio for his birthday."
>
> Q: "Dad, what does 'better half' mean?"
>
> A: "Just what she says."
>
> Bruce: "Joe dislocated his jaw and shoulder during the Sanford game."
>
> Virginia B.: "Horrible! I didn't know Joe played football."
>
> Bruce: "He doesn't. He's a cheerleader."
>
> And, finally . . . "You had some fresh shrimps here last week," began the purchaser.
>
> "Yes, ma'am," interrupted the market man apologetically, "but I fired both of them."

Soon after writing and publishing these bon mots, west Orange high school students would transfer to the collegiate-gothic splendor of the new Lakeview High School, overlooking Lake Apopka. "The new high school building" in Winter Garden "is among the finest in the state," professor William Fremont Blackman wrote in his *History of Orange County* in 1927, the year the school opened. West Orange pioneer Luther Fuller Tilden, then 93, donated 17 acres of land for the campus and was thanked in elegant letters at the left front corner of the building. A matching plaque honors the school's revered principal, Mrs. J.S. Kirton, who led Lakeview for 30 years. Signs on the West Orange Trail point to the two-story brick building, now part of Lakeview Middle School.

In downtown Orlando, the building fever of the 1920s had produced another kind of hall for learning, the city's first major public library. Late in 1921, the city tapped architect Murry

S. King to draw up tentative plans for what would become the Albertson Public Library. In a few years King would also design the nearby neoclassic 1927 courthouse building that now houses the Orange County Regional History Center.

The inspiration and the collection of books for the Albertson sprang from two sources: an Orlando women's group and an ex-New York City police officer. The group, Orlando's Sorosis Club, had been organized in 1893 with the purpose of bringing together "a congenial set of women who were interested in literature," according to Eve Bacon's history of Orlando. The club is credited with starting Orlando's first circulating library, operating first from members' homes and for a time from rooms in the three-story brick armory building, built in 1893. Several years later, the Sorosis Club and its lending library moved to nearby quarters at 34 East Pine Street, where a brass plaque pays homage to these women who put books in the hands of others for free. The Sorosis lending library formed part of the nucleus of the Albertson Public Library.

Much of the library's initial collection also came from the man whose name would go above the door: Captain Charles L. Albertson. Born in 1856, Albertson had joined the New York City police force in 1879 and "was rapidly advanced to the highest position and was an excellent officer," according to E.H. Gore's 1949 history of Orlando. He retired in 1905 and came to Orlando in 1913. The good law officer was also an avid book collector, and he offered to give 12,000 volumes to the city, if it would build a library to house them. The books weighed 40,000 pounds and were valued at $75,000.

The library opened in November 1923 with a total of 20,000 volumes from the Albertson and Sorosis collections. In contrast, by 2001 the Orange County Library System circulated about 4 million items a year. The system's flagship library, the big Orlando building that replaced the 1923 Albertson, is visited by more than a million people annually. There, the Albertson Room continues to honor the New York police captain who bestowed his beloved books on his new home in the sun.

Not all Orlandoans could enjoy the captain's gift, however. Held by the grip of segregation, the doors of the city's major library were closed to members of the African-American community until the mid-1960s, as were most other public facilities. But the vision of a library for black residents was wide open in the early 1920s, says Lorelei Anderson-Francis, who has led efforts to recognize that library's vital heritage. Jones High School, Orlando's traditionally black high school that was then on Parramore Street, "was the unofficial library for a long time," Anderson-Francis says. Teachers there "were collecting things and praying that one day they would have a library, anywhere." Others shared the teachers' vision, including Olive Brumbach, founding director of the Albertson Library.

On June 11, 1924, less than a year after the Albertson opened, a newspaper story noted the debut of its first branch "in what was the rectory of the Negro Episcopal church" on Terry Avenue, near West Church Street. It would be called the Booker T. Washington branch—to honor the great black educator, who had died in 1915—and it would have a substation at Jones High School, the report continued. "The library is starting off with an equipment of more than 1,200 volumes, placed in two reading rooms and a reference room. The children's room is particularly attractive and well-equipped," the story said.

The first librarian at the Booker T. Washington library, Mrs. Eddie Cromartie Jackson, was a graduate of Morris Brown University in Atlanta. She initially worked also as a schoolteacher during the day and managed the branch after school and on weekends. Her starting salary was $30 a month. K.B. Taylor, the public-health nurse who gave shots to all the area children and otherwise worked to keep them healthy, assisted in activities that included popular story hours. During the first six weeks the library was open, 300 people registered for library cards. By early 1929, the number had climbed to 2,142.

The library's special mission to serve children was apparent from its earliest years. Mrs. Jackson wrote in the 1920s in a flier preserved in the library archives:

> Parents, manifest more interest in the library, because it is an asset to the community. A person cannot travel everywhere, meet people of all types, converse with men of all minds, unless he reads. . . . Teach your children to appreciate images of beauty, and the emotions are appealed to through ennobling sentiments.

At a 2001 fete to honor the history of the Booker T. Washington Library, Dorothy T. Johnson of nearby Celebration said she found it remarkable that in the 1920s a then-small city such as Orlando had a library for black residents. "I didn't grow up in Orlando, but I do remember 1924," said Johnson, then 86. Most often, "people of color were not allowed in city libraries—there was no access at all." The celebration Johnson attended ended with the unveiling of a historical marker bearing words of the late Arthur "Pappy" Kennedy, Orlando's first black City Council member, elected in 1973: "Work, study and read . . . read everything you can find to read."

It's very likely some of the youngsters who checked out books from the Booker T. Washington Library in the mid-1920s also gleaned inspiration from one of the most glamorous figures ever to spend time in Orlando—the first American woman to earn an international pilot's license. Nope, it wasn't Amelia Earhart, although, like Earhart, she was young, good-looking, and had great flair—a woman famous actresses would compete to portray. Her name was Bessie Coleman.

Like Earhart, Coleman died tragically during a flight in 1926, but under much more public circumstances, in Jacksonville, Florida. One of three large funeral services for her took place in Orlando. "Funeral for Negro Aviatrix," read the tiny notice in the *Orlando Morning Sentinel*.

There was nothing small about Coleman's spirit, though, or the remarkable story of her short life. She was born January 26, 1892, in Atlanta, Texas, a small town close to the borders of Louisiana and Arkansas. Her mother, Susan, had probably been born a slave. Soon the family moved to a larger town, Waxahachie, where Susan Coleman worked as a housekeeper for a white family. Though she could not read or write, she made sure her nine children did.

Bessie, a clever, lively child, got the job of reading to her younger siblings after dinner. The Bible came first—mother's orders—but Bessie liked best to read tales of black heroes such as Harriet Tubman or Booker T. Washington. She also read fiction, especially *Uncle Tom's Cabin*, although she saw the characters of Topsy and Uncle Tom as exactly what she did not want her life to be. Years later, when she was raising money for a flight school to train black pilots, she told reporters she was going to make "Uncle Tom's cabin into a hangar."

In 1915 Coleman headed to Chicago, where her older brothers lived. She worked first as a manicurist and then as a restaurant manager. But it was after her brothers returned from

Sizzle and Fizzle in the Roaring Twenties

World War I that her life reached a turning point. They told her of the lack of prejudice in France, and she heard tales of wartime aviation. Her mind was made up: Bessie Coleman would learn to fly. Undaunted after flight schools in this country turned her down, she made it to France in 1920, with the help of black philanthropists including Robert Abbott, the founder of the *Chicago Defender*, and became the first American woman and the first black American to obtain an international pilot's license, on June 15, 1921.

During a speaking tour through Florida in early 1926, Coleman met an Orlando couple, the Reverend Hezakiah Keith Hill and his wife, Viola Tillinghast Hill, respected community activists. She became close to the couple and stayed with them at the parsonage of Orlando's Mount Zion Missionary Baptist Institutional Church. "For Bessie the spacious house on shady, tree-lined Washington Street became the center of her life, the idyllic home she had never had," Coleman's biographer, Doris Rich, writes.

Coleman had lost her first airplane during a crash, and she was purchasing a used Curtiss JN-4, or "Jenny," from a Texas company in installments. Edwin Beeman, a white member of a leading Orlando family who was fascinated by aviation, is said to have given Coleman the money for the final installment on her plane. (The Beemans are the folks of chewing-gum fame.)

With her plane paid for and on the way from Texas, flown by white mechanic William D. Wills, Coleman headed to Jacksonville for a flying exhibition. During a rehearsal flight on April 30, with Wills and Coleman both on board, the plane spun out of control. Coleman was flung to her death; Wills died in the crash. More than 5,000 attended services for Coleman in Jacksonville, including schoolchildren who had heard her speak only the day before she was killed.

Then her body was put on the train to Orlando. The service that followed on the morning of Monday, May 3, was one of the largest Mount Zion Missionary Baptist had ever seen. After it was over, mourners, led by Viola Hill, who would accompany the body to Chicago, crowded the Orlando train station to say goodbye to an American heroine. "As the body of Miss Coleman was being raised into the baggage car, en route to its final resting place," one report said, "more than 500 voices, representing the colored population of the city, hummed sweetly, 'My Country, 'Tis of Thee.' "

About the same time black Orlandoans were saying goodbye to the glamorous pilot, an area resident was making another kind of transportation history. Hoyle Pounds put American farmers on a roll with his rubber-tired farm tractor.

After engineering studies and a football career at the University of Florida, Pounds had opened a garage in Ocoee in 1914. In a few years he moved to Winter Garden, where he started a Ford dealership. By 1918 he was Florida's first Ford Motor Company tractor dealer, Orlandoan Henry Swanson says in his important book *Countdown for Agriculture in Orange County, Florida*.

The wave of land speculation that was pulling people into the state hit Pounds's business along with everyone else's. In 1919 Pounds sold eight tractors, but by 1926, the year he put up the brick building on Plant Street that's still a feature of Winter Garden, his agency was selling more than 40 a year.

Those tractors moved on metal wheels with metal cleats that grabbed into the soil. Highway building was bustling in Central Florida, and farmers and citrus growers now had to traverse these newly paved roads. The result was that the metal cleats chewed up the pavement, gaining tractors the name "highway eaters." Faced with expensively hacked-up roadways, officials passed laws forbidding the metal wheels from crossing the highways. And tractor owners complained to Hoyle Pounds.

From Oklahoma, Pounds ordered some large, hard rubber tires designed for oil-drilling equipment. After considerable experimentation, he realized that the gear ratio to the drive shaft would have to be changed. Tire-clad wheels turned at a faster rate than the old metal wheels, moving on top of the soil rather than digging into it.

After all the details had been tested for several months, Pounds applied for and was granted Patent Number 1662208 on March 13, 1928, for his rim and lug design for airless tires. The use of rubber tires not only made tractors faster, it increased their mobility. "Pounds' invention 'ushered in' the use of rubber tires on virtually all movable farm equipment," Swanson writes.

Still active into his 80s, Pounds led the Winter Garden volunteer fire department for 40 years. Before he died in 1981, he received many state and national honors for his work to transform the old "highway eaters."

As inventions such as Pounds's tractor transformed American life, Orlando too was changing. What had been a little country village was becoming "a real metropolitan city," Carl Dann wrote near the close of the 1920s:

> I watched the man on horseback light the first gas lights at sundown; then I saw electric lights come in. . . . I watched the streets turn from grass to sandy thoroughfares, then into clay, and finally into brick and hard pavement. I watched the people celebrate and wonder when we had the first telephone.

Now, on January 11, 1927, Orlandoans were ready to celebrate again, in what would be one of land-boom's last hurrahs. The new Atlantic Coast Line Depot was to be "the scene of elaborate festivities" that day, a news story had proclaimed. Nearly 50 railroad executives were expected to join city dignitaries to open the new station on Sligh Boulevard, built at a cost of nearly $500,000 and "said to be one of the most beautiful in the South." It still stands and serves as Orlando's Amtrak station, one the area's landmarks noted in the *Guide to Florida's Historic Architecture*, but also one of its least appreciated.

In 1927, the Sligh Boulevard station was the equivalent to Orlando International Airport today. There retirees and rogues, matrons and mavericks, would step down into the City Beautiful from the cool shade of a streamlined railroad car. They would blink into the blinding bright sun up at the white walls of the station, where an arch of letters above the station door made their destination unmistakable—ORLANDO, in sweeping capitals, perhaps the most beautiful public rendering of the city's name. Each letter was hand-designed by the station's architect, A.M. Griffin of the Atlantic Coast Line.

The railroad's top brass had sent Griffin to travel the Pacific Coast to study the Spanish colonial missions for inspiration. True, the Spanish colonists had not left a similar trail of stucco missions in Florida, but the state's name and climate—and Spanish heritage—seemed reason enough for the choice of the Mission Revival style popular in the 1920s. And so, with its twin bell towers, arches, and tile roof, an homage to historic buildings in San Francisco,

Santa Barbara, Carmel, and other California locales became the Atlantic Coast Line's very Pacific-looking gift to Orlando. The station remains the most sophisticated and largest example of Mission Revival architecture in the area.

On that January afternoon, Orlandoans drove their Model "T"s south of Lake Lucerne to welcome the station warmly. The crowd of 6,000 was so large that extra traffic officers labored to manage the hundreds of cars crowding the blocks around the building, the *Morning Sentinel* reported afterward. The interior of the station overflowed with potted palms and flowers, fragrant congratulatory gifts from civic groups. The Lions Club quartet sang, two bands played, and exuberant speakers hailed a "new era of progress and expansion."

But even as the crowd celebrated, the bubble had begun to burst, pierced by a monster Miami-area hurricane in the fall of 1926 that gave Northern investors cold feet about warm Florida. Revenue from membership dues at the Orlando Chamber of Commerce plunged from $100,000 in 1926 to just $27,000 by mid-March 1927. More booms and good times were ahead for Orlando, but it may be the graceful letters that spell its name at the train station never looked down on as grand a day as that winter afternoon when the shiny-new, flower-filled depot on Sligh Boulevard gave to the incoming visitor, in the newspaper's words, "a first impression of the City Beautiful destined to be lasting and entrancing."

Chapter Seven

INNOVATORS, ARTISTS, COWBOYS, AND SOLDIERS

As the 1920s receded and the Great Depression descended over Orlando, the high-throttle pace of land-boom days slowed to a steady rhythm. Yet the City Beautiful had been changed forever, not just by the new buildings in its skyline but by its increasing role as a tourist destination and a haven for folks from "up North" who sought a new life in the sunshine. The hubbub was over, but Orlando was on the move. During the 1930s, Orange County's population grew from almost 50,000 to more than 70,000.

Many residents worked in the citrus industry. Orange County growers had recovered from the Great Freeze of 1894–1895, but by 1930, they were suffering not only from the land boom's bust but also from the repercussions of Mediterranean fruit-fly discovery in Orlando in 1929. The eradication campaign that followed meant trouble for the fresh-fruit business, and some Central Florida citrus leaders, including Dr. Philip Phillips, started thinking more seriously about orange juice. In fact, in the years before World War II, it was Doc himself who made Florida's "liquid sunshine" synonymous with a boost to good health.

At one time, Dr. Phillips's enterprises grew and sold 100 million oranges a year, more than any other citrus business in the world. In 1928, he had opened the world's largest citrus-packing house 10 miles outside Orlando, where a train depot bore his name. In the late 1920s, he owned more acreage planted to citrus than any other person in the state. Faced with the fruit-fly crisis in the days before refrigeration, Doc turned his attention to solving a problem that had bedeviled the industry. Orange juice may have been good for you, but it didn't taste very good in a can. It had a metallic tinge and was in great popular disfavor.

Phillips bought a large building in Orlando at Princeton Street beside the Atlantic Coast Line Railroad tracks, converted it into a plant for processing citrus products, and put together a team to build a market for canned juice by improving its taste. Between 1929 and 1931, Phillips's researchers ran countless experiments, often setting out batches of fruit and juice on the roof to see how they responded to outdoor exposure and incubation. Eventually they came up with a "flash" pasteurization process that greatly improved the taste and appeal of single-strength orange juice, and Phillips followed up with a five-state marketing blitz that supplied grocery shoppers with free samples of chilled, canned juice.

Although the orange-juice frozen concentrate revolution was years away, at the end of World War II, Dr. Phillips's processing breakthroughs in the early 1930s "helped establish the confidence in citrus juice products that later paved the way" toward popular acceptance of such products as concentrate and packaged, chilled juice, agricultural historian Henry Swanson writes.

Phillips was even better at marketing as he was at innovation. The labels on his juice cans read: "Drink Dr. Phillips' orange juice because the Doc says it's good for you." His medical title was mysterious. According to one story, the French government had given him an honorary degree for letting the Red Cross use a chateau he owned as a field hospital during World War I. Research by Dr. Phillips Incorporated officials suggests that he went to medical school in New York and briefly practiced in Tennessee. Apparently, he never practiced medicine in Florida. No matter. In the early 1930s, the American Medical Association's Council on Foods issued its seal of acceptance for all of Dr. Phillips's canned products. After that, the labels bore the seal "Accepted American Medical Ass'n Committee on Foods." Like the name "Dr. Phillips," the AMA imprimatur helped seal in the public mind the association between processed citrus products and good health.

Dr. Phillips was responsible for one of the most delightfully quirky episodes in Orlando history when he imported an unlikely 67-year-old drought-buster in a parched April of 1939. Desperate citrus growers in the Florida cities of Frostproof and Sebring had already called on Miss Lillie Stoate, a Mississippi rainmaker, for help before she reached Orlando at Doc's request. It had rained in both places after her arrival. In a world weary of depressing war rumblings in Europe and drought at home, Miss Lillie was happy, front-page news.

The good lady aimed to "project herself into the firmament" to bring the rain the citrus groves needed so badly, news reports said. Her method was to sit in a vigil at the center of a drought drama—in Orlando's case, near Dr. Phillips's headquarters by Sand Lake. She occupied herself in these vigils by reading the paper, eating strawberries or just plain sitting. "Though she was a good Christian," she told one reporter, she didn't pray for rain. "I just have the power to bring rain, and I can't explain it," she said. Headlines from the day after Miss Lillie sat by Sand Lake testified to her powers: "Rainmaker's Charms Work in Orlando" and "Rainmaker Brings 'Pennies from Heaven.' " "Heavy rains and showers had poured down on Central Florida the evening and day after her vigil, putting the "prolonged drought on the run."

Another newsworthy lady, Margaret "Mickey" Ekdahl, enthralled Orlando at the start of the Depression decade when she became Orlando's own Miss America. Born Agnes Margrit Elisabeth Ekdahl in Eslov, Sweden, in 1912, she had moved with her family to Orlando in 1926. Ekdahl was more than just pretty: Pictures show a haunting quality in her eyes, perhaps the same hint of Scandinavian mystery that helped make Greta Garbo a legend. The Orlando girl must have been compared with Garbo, Hollywood's reigning queen about the time the press dubbed Ekdahl the Viking Queen. Like Garbo, Ekdahl is in the Scandinavian Hall of Fame. And like Garbo, Ekdahl wanted her privacy—but she wasn't blessed with a long life in which to savor it. America's sweetheart of 1930 was dead before the close of 1932.

The Atlantic City pageant didn't exist during Ekdahl's year in the spotlight: It was shelved from 1928 through 1932 because of the Great Depression. Miss Ekdahl had entered the Miami National Beauty Contest; her official title was "America's Sweetheart." But the national press of the day called her Miss America, and so did the folks back home.

As Miss Florida, she had originally placed third in the Miami contest. But she had a powerful champion in Orlando booster R.B. Brossier, an owner, with his twin brother J.C., of Orlando's afternoon daily, the *Evening Reporter-Star*. After Ekdahl's death, R.B. Brossier wrote a tribute recalling the days when, as a schoolgirl, she worked in the tearoom of the Yowell-Drew department store. "I remarked to her, 'Some day, Miss Cinderella, we shall make you America's Beauty Queen.' " In 1930, he had the chance.

ORLANDO

After the Miami contest, pageant officials discovered that the winner, Miss Texas, was divorced and the runner-up, Miss California, was actually from Oklahoma. They apparently learned the distressing details from publisher R.B. Brossier of Orlando, who said he had proof, including a copy of Miss Texas' marriage license. The result: Mickey Ekdahl of Florida was proclaimed America's Sweetheart. Brossier's bombshells had made his Orlando Cinderella a queen. She was only 18 years old.

Ekdahl was dispatched on a publicity-filled, 10-week national tour that stretched into eight months. She gave interviews, judged beauty contests, endorsed products from cars to cosmetics, met Gary Cooper, and was offered a Hollywood career herself. She turned it all down. Instead, she returned to live in Orlando, where she worked in Dickson & Ives department store. Orlandoans were shocked to read of her death in late 1932, after surgery at Orlando General Hospital following an attack of peritonitis. Nearly 2,500 people came to Carey Hand Funeral Home's chapel to pay their respects, "to say their farewells to the girl they knew and loved," the *Reporter-Star* said.

Time has dimmed Mickey Ekdahl's flash of fame, but she hasn't been forgotten. After all these years, family members have said, someone—they don't know who—still puts flowers on the grave of the girl with the haunting eyes.

If some days were sad or tough during the Depression, longtime Orlandoans treasure plenty of happy memories as well. After graduating from Orlando High in 1931, future Orlando civic leader and history booster Joseph Wittenstein was working to gather money for college when he saw a way to boost his savings and have some fun.

Hearing that Charlie Boulanger's popular dance orchestra was booked for a six-week gig in Miami, Wittenstein and two buddies talked the band into playing Orlando and rented the Coliseum, the big hall on North Orange Avenue that had been built in the 1920s. The young producers' greatest triumph was an appearance by Cab Calloway and his orchestra, then a sensation at Harlem's Cotton Club. Booking a black band for a white audience was a daring venture in Jim Crow days in the South. But with the help of Henry Sadler, the head bellman at the San Juan Hotel (and a man who knew how to get things done), the young promoters found lodging for Calloway and his band and hired extra security. They had no problems, though; a happy crowd danced to New York's most fashionable sounds.

In 1932, the publishers of the *Orlando Morning Sentinel* and the *Evening Reporter-Star* had in mind even bigger star power than Cab Calloway to dispel the city's Depression gloom. Shortly after Thanksgiving, the papers announced that Santa himself would appear in the city to help folks forget their troubles. Back then, the big guy had substantial star power. He was advertised to speak nightly on the radio, on Orlando's WDBO, but live appearances weren't an everyday thing.

Santa would "take our thoughts off depression in its real and in its imagined aspects," an announcement said. Front-page articles, "special by Polar Bear Telegraph Inc.," traced a world tour by the "Cheer King" as he made his way to the Sunshine State from his North Pole home. "Santa Claus, Orlando Bound, Pays Short Visit to Russia," read the headline of one piece with a Leningrad dateline, laced with sly Depression-era political commentary:

> Greeted by all the officials of the land of the Soviets, Comrade Santa Clausky, friend of all good little communists, arrived here today bound for the United

States of America in general, and in particular for Orlandovitch, Floridisky. . . . A conference between Mr. Clausky and Mr. Stalin, rumor has it, has led Comrade Stalin to feel the first faint flickers of the Christmas spirit.

Soon, bold type announced that Santa would arrive in Orlando on December 7 at the fairgrounds, then downtown, west of what's now the Bob Carr Performing Arts Centre. There Santa would serve up, for free, 5,000 hot dogs and 5,000 "bottles of pop" and "many thousand pieces of gum" for the thousands of boys and girls he expected to see. What's more, he was going to make quite an entrance. "Dear Boys and Girls," he wrote. "I will land by parachute at the fairgrounds around 4:30 p.m. (weather permitting). Please meet me there. Yours, Santa Claus."

Youngsters were to meet by 4:00 p.m. at Orange Avenue and Jackson Street downtown and form a promenade to the fairgrounds, in an event expected to "eclipse practically anything the city has ever seen in the way of a child's parade." The next day, a headline reported great success. "Orlando Children Wildly Cheer Arrival of Santa, Fairgrounds Teem with Action," it read, above an international headline the likes of which we won't see again: "Cuspidors Hurled at Wild Melee in Reich."

More than 7,000 children had been on hand to greet the old gent on his leap from the blue. They had paraded to see him, thrilled to get a free hot dog washed down with soda, maybe some chewing gum, too, and a glimpse of Santa Claus appearing from the sky. Not pricey treats to be sure, but as the newspaper stated when it announced Santa's appearance:

> Money is only good to the extent that it will buy the things needed to make people comfortable and happy. . . . Central Florida people have been favored in so many ways, are in so much better circumstances than other localities and celebrate under such a happy environment that they should enter the season with high hopes and a joyful spirit.

Nowhere is the spirit of Santa more welded to Orlando's past than at Christmas, Florida, the east Orange County community that sprang from pioneer roots when soldiers founded a fort on December 25, 1837. Since 1892, there's been a post office at Christmas, and for more than 60 of those years, a Tucker has been in charge. Lizzie Tucker got the job in 1916, and her daughter-in-law Juanita took over in 1932 and stayed on the job for more than 40 years. For the 1934 holidays, Juanita Tucker began the practice of putting a hand-stamped Christmas tree on envelopes. Called a cachet, the little green trees are as much a part of Christmas, Florida, postal lore as the community's treasured postmark. In the weeks between Thanksgiving and December 25, packages arrive at the post office in east Orange County from Italy, France, and other locales around the world, bearing cards to be postmarked and mailed from Christmas.

In 1932, when Juanita Tucker began her tenure, the Christmas post office was located in a two-story frame building on Fort Christmas Road, where patrons' postal boxes were wooden pigeonholes. About 1937, the post office moved to the homey, one-story building with a small porch that appears in many photos of the Christmas post office from the 1940s and

1950s. The building has been moved from its original site and now stands at the corner of Colonial Drive (State Road 50) and Fort Christmas Road. Near it stands a life-size creche, a large tinsel-clad tree, and a much-photographed plaque that says: "The permanent Christmas tree at Christmas Florida is the symbol of love and good will; the Christmas Spirit every day in the year."

While Juanita Tucker began building a Central Florida tradition in the 1930s in a very real place named Christmas, the architect James Gamble Rogers was busy crafting houses in the Orlando area that might have sprung from the pages of a storybook. Rogers, who died in 1990 at 89 after a 60-plus-year career, was James Gamble Rogers II. His uncle, the first James Gamble Rogers, is the fellow with an entry in the *Columbia Encyclopedia* ("American architect, b. Kentucky") who was responsible for the collegiate gothic and colonial-revival styles of architecture so popular on American campuses built in the 1920s through 1940s.

Born in 1901, Central Florida's James Gamble Rogers moved as a boy to Daytona Beach. After college at Dartmouth, he worked and studied in his father's Daytona architectural office until he opened a branch of that business in Winter Park in 1928. In 1935, he started his own firm, now Rogers, Lovelock & Fritz (RLF). In Winter Park, Rogers shaped much of the campus of Rollins College, as his uncle had done at Yale. His work there and the Florida Supreme Court building in Tallahassee count among his notable achievements, but it is his Central Florida homes, from cottages to mansions, that his admirers value most. His favorites, he once said, included the home on Laurel Avenue at Marks Street in Orlando he built for Dr. L.C. Ingram in the late 1930s. French provincial with a touch of Tudor, it has an almost imperceptible, intentional dip in its roof line and looks as if it was built well before the twentieth century.

In 1932, Robert Bruce Barbour, the inventor of laundry bluing, asked Rogers to create a house for him on the shores of Lake Osceola in Winter Park. The result, considered the crown jewel of Gamble Rogers's houses, is still called the Barbour house, although it has had several owners in the decades since. It is also called Casa Feliz, and to build it the architect turned to materials with stories of their own.

For the home's foot-thick walls, Rogers scooped up the bricks from the old Orlando Armory, built in 1886 and torn down in 1932. Through them, Casa Feliz became a link to the larger community's past, the center of life in the days when Orlando had called itself the "Phenomenal City." At the Armory farmer's market in the late nineteenth century, 40 vendors had opened for business six days a week in stalls they rented for $5 a month.

Over the vintage bricks, Rogers put a roof of tiles handmade by workers in Spain in the time-honored way, by forming the clay over their thighs to shape the curved tile. At the end of the 1920s, the tiles had been shipped to Cuba, where department-store magnate J.C. Penney obtained them for a winter home he planned to build in Jacksonville. But Penney's plans were dampened by the Depression, and after he abandoned the tiles in Jacksonville, Rogers managed to acquire them for Casa Feliz. Such attention to materials and detail characterized his work. When Barbour returned from a trip and first saw his house, he found Rogers himself up on a ladder, chipping away at an archway to make it look a little more timeless, like something fashioned from dreams rather than blueprints.

Continued on page 129

Native peoples called Timucuans inhabited north-central Florida at the time of European exploration. In 1564, artist Jacques Le Moyne accompanied a French expedition and made sketches and later paintings of Florida natives. In 1591 a German artist, Theodor de Bry, translated Le Moyne's images into engravings. Here, Timucuans smoke a variety of game on a rack. (Florida Photographic Collection.)

The first inhabitants of the Florida peninsula were Paleoindians who arrived thousands of years before European explorers. Archaeologists found this small figure in an Indian mound by the Wacissa River in Florida's Panhandle in 1936. (Florida Photographic Collection.)

The traditional dress of Seminole men included a turban of sorts and one or several bandannas or neckerchiefs. This photo was likely taken in the early 1890s. (Florida Photographic Collection.)

"Osceola, the Black Drink Crier, a Warrior of Great Distinction" (1838), by George Catlin (1796–1872), is in the Smithsonian Institution. "I have painted him precisely in the costume in which he stood for his picture, even to a string and a trinket," Catlin wrote. Perhaps history's most famous Floridian, Osceola was descended from Scottish, Creek, and African ancestors. (Florida Photographic Collection.)

Massacre of the Whites by the Indians and Blacks in Florida.

The above is intended to represent the horrid Massacre of the Whites in Florida, in December **1835**, and January, February, March and April **1836**, when near Four Hundred (including women and children) fell victims to the barbarity of the Negroes and Indians.

Blacks, Native Americans, and whites all played a major role in Florida's Seminole wars, which were fueled in part by Southern planters' desire to recapture slaves who had fled into Florida. The bottom of this political drawing from 1836 reads, "The above is intended to present the horrid Massacre of the Whites in Florida, in December 1835, and January, February, March and April 1836, when near Four Hundred (including women and children) fell victims to the barbarity of the Negroes and Indians." (Florida Photographic Collection.)

Born in Sweden, Kena Fries moved with her family to Orlando as a small child in 1873. This photo was taken in 1888, when she was about 20. Her father, surveyor J. Otto Fries, was one of early Orlando's most learned and respected men. In 1938, she published a history titled Orlando: In the Long, Long Ago, and Now. *(Historical Society of Central Florida, Incorporated.)*

This image of a Seminole leader is identified in the Florida Photographic Collection as Chief Billy Bowlegs in 1852, the year he journeyed to Washington and other Eastern cities. A New York reporter wrote that the chief was "about 40 years of age and was clad in a calico frock, leggings and a belt or two and a sort of short cloak. On his head he wore a kind of turban . . . surmounted by a profusion of black ostrich feathers."

Traditional Seminole dress after about 1900 featured elaborate patchwork patterns, made on sewing machines. In 1900, Orlandoan J. Otto Fries ventured to the Seminoles' south Florida reservation to take the first census there. This photo was probably taken in the 1930s. (Historical Society of Central Florida, Incorporated.)

In early Orlando lore, the Council Oak was said to have been a meeting place for Osceola, Coacoochee, and other native leaders in Seminole war days. It was struck by lightning in the 1880s. This image from about 1910 looks east from South Ferncreek Avenue, near the site of a historical marker placed in 1970. (Historical Society of Central Florida, Incorporated.)

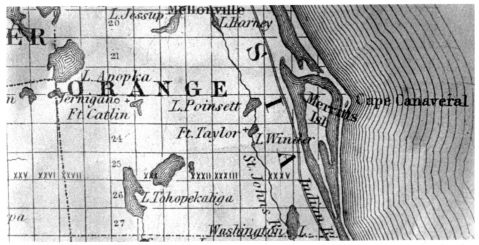

J.H. Colton's 1855 map of Florida, one of the best-known early maps of the peninsula after statehood, shows the settlement of Jernigan, as well as Fort Gatlin, the origins of Orlando. (Florida Photographic Collection.)

This 1880s photo has become an icon of pioneer days in Orlando, where the "gator wrestler" has been transformed into a statue and even an image on city buses. The Orange County Regional History Center identifies the man on the reptile as Bunk Baxter; members of the Yates family have said he is Bud Yates. Both men no doubt brought specimens of wild Florida to town on market days. Researchers have pointed out that the reptile in the photo is most likely a crocodile, not an alligator, because of its pointy snout. (Historical Society of Central Florida, Incorporated.)

Early African-American residents of Orlando included Uncle Mose Paine, a former slave. His wife, Ellen, prepared meals at the Duke Hall rooming house on East Pine Street. This photo is likely from the 1880s. (Historical Society of Central Florida, Incorporated.)

Mrs. Martha Tyler, daughter of pioneer Aaron Jernigan, unveiling marker, March 27, 1924.

On March 27, 1924, Martha Jernigan Tyler, then 85, was honored as the last survivor of Fort Gatlin at ceremonies to place a historical marker near the fort's site. Born in 1839, she could recall Orlando's earliest pioneer days. (Historical Society of Central Florida, Incorporated.)

This 1842 map of the territory of Florida shows Mosquito County, the huge precursor of Orange County. Orlando became the county seat of Orange in 1857. (Florida Photographic Collection.)

This photo has long been identified as Jacob Summerlin (1820–1893), a towering figure in the history of Orlando and the state as a whole. In 1949 a group of Orlando residents placed a large copy of the photo in the Orange County Courthouse to honor Summerlin. Some relatives have disputed its authenticity. The gentleman resembles other pictures of Summerlin; perhaps a photographer persuaded him to pose with pipe and whip as symbols of his roots on the Florida range. (Historical Society of Central Florida, Incorporated.)

Jacob Summerlin's contributions to Orlando included the Summerlin Hotel near Lake Eola, a center of activity in the young city. A sign at the desk in the hotel's early years offered to pay "10 cents hard cash" to any guest who could produce a mosquito actually caught in the hotel. (Historical Society of Central Florida, Incorporated.)

Angeline Mizell, the widow of slain Orange County Sheriff David Mizell, sat for a portrait with her children, probably in the 1890s. Pictured are, from left to right, (standing) John Thomas, Lulu Amanda, Joshua, and Della; (seated) Sarah Ann, Angeline, and Mollie. Another son died in 1883. Sheriff Mizell's ambush and death by gunshots in 1870 were part of the bloody Barber-Mizell feud. (Historical Society of Central Florida, Incorporated.)

Photographer H.A. Abercromby took this portrait of an African-American church group in Orlando or Winter Park in the late 1890s. Newspaperman Mahlon Gore's 1884 population count included 504 African Americans in a total of 1,666 residents. (Florida Photographic Collection.)

About 1882, photographer Stanley Morrow captured the view looking west on Orlando's Pine Street, one of the city's main business corridors. Fire destroyed much of the business district in January 1884. (Florida Photographic Collection.)

Orlandoans celebrated the Fourth of July with a horse-powered parade on West Church Street about 1886, after the arrival of the railroad had fired up the area's growth and Orlando began to call itself "the Phenomenal City." The parade is about to turn north onto Orange Avenue. The horizontal band across the bottom is from an early identification label pasted on the photo. (Florida Photographic Collection.)

Responding to recruiting ads in England, younger sons of the English gentry arrived in the Orlando area in the late 1880s and early 1890s to try out the life of a gentleman citrus grower. Many of the members of the "English colony" settled in the Lake Conway area.

A photographer snapped some unidentified members of Orlando's English colony with an African-American woman who likely was the family's housekeeper. When the Great Freeze hit the area in late December 1894 and February 1895, many of the colony fled quickly.

The hospitable Leslie Pell-Clarke entertained many of Orlando's English settlers at his large Orlando home, a far cry from the world in which his family circulated in Newport, Rhode Island, and Westchester County, New York. In 1900, Pell-Clarke gave his home to the Episcopal Church to be used as the bishop's residence. (Historical Society of Central Florida, Incorporated.)

This view looking west on Church Street about 1886 shows the South Florida Railroad station and the perhaps single, mule-drawn car of the Orlando Street Railway, which later ran on a track. N.L. Mills owned the car, which was ruled by his son Ernest, a town institution who answered only to his own inner voice when it came to a schedule. The car might disappear for hours, but Ernest Mills also endeared himself to Orlando ladies by picking up groceries for them and even taking a bit of ribbon or lace to a store to be matched. (Florida Photographic Collection.)

This wedding party was photographed in front of the Tremont Hotel at Main (Magnolia) and East Church Streets. Begun in 1895 by James Wilmott, an English sea captain who arrived in town in 1883, the Tremont lasted until 1956. (Historical Society of Central Florida, Incorporated.)

The first Orange County Fair took place on the north side of Lake Eola in 1886, according to Eve Bacon's history of the city. The wooden exposition building stood on the present-day site of the Rosalind Club. The park also boasted a race track in the late 1880s. The Great Freeze of the 1890s put a temporary end to the fairs, which revived about 1911. (Florida Photographic Collection.)

When Orange County's new red-brick courthouse debuted in 1892, some residents wondered what in the world little Orlando was doing with such a huge building. The postcard shows the 1911 Confederate monument in the intersection at right before its 1917 move to Lake Eola Park. (Historical Society of Central Florida, Incorporated.)

Until the devastating freeze of 1894–1895, Central Florida citrus growers relied only on location to protect their groves from cold. As the citrus industry began to recover in the early twentieth century, growers used heaters, some fueled by kerosene, to fend off freezes. In this undated photo, a citrus man keeps watch during an Orlando-area cold spell. (Historical Society of Central Florida, Incorporated.)

The chance to hunt and fish even in winter made life in Orlando appealing to many sportsmen from the North and from England, too, in the late 1880s through early 1900s. This well-armed and well-dressed party is ready to head into the palmetto woods. (Historical Society of Central Florida, Incorporated.)

Photographed in Tampa about 1900, Orlando boosters touted the city's advantages. The "no insects" claim had a serious subtext. An epidemic of mosquito-borne yellow fever had hit Florida hard in 1888, but Orlando had managed to escape without a single case being reported in the city. (Historical Society of Central Florida, Incorporated.)

Orlando businessman S.G. Dolive is at the wheel of a fine vehicle decked out for an automobile parade about 1911, when the city staged a grand procession that toured the city. Note that in early automobiles, the driver was on the right side of the vehicle. (Historical Society of Central Florida, Incorporated.)

Arriving in 1913 from Pittsburgh, Israel Shader brought the first Torah to the Orlando area. The Shader family bought an orange grove in the Fairvilla area. The daughters of Israel and Rose Shader and their children posed for this portrait about 1917. The women are, from left to right, Esther Shader Wittenstein, Fannie Shader Meitin, and Sarah Shader Miller. The children are Ruth Meitin, Joe W. Wittenstein, Ralph Meitin, and Lilli Ann Miller. (Florida Photographic Collection.)

The German-American settlement of Gotha a few miles west of Orlando drew pioneering horticulturist Henry Nehrling and his family to the area about 1902, after he bought land there in 1884. At his Gotha gardens, Nehrling gathered plants from around the world and did much to build the foundations of Florida's tropical-plant industry. (Courtesy of Richard Nehrling.)

Vacationers enjoy the charms of Clay Springs, now Wekiwa Springs, in 1900. The photo says "The Grasmere 'Automobile' at Clay Springs, Fla., March 31, 1900." Developed in the railroad-powered land boom of the 1880s, Clay Springs was long a popular picnic spot for Orlandoans and a vacation destination for Northerners. In the 1880s an Iowa newspaperman named J.D. Smith built a three-story hotel there, the Ton-Ya-Wa-Tha, which local lore said meant "healing waters." He also laid out plans for a town called Sulphur Springs, but the name didn't catch on, and the area continued to be known as Clay Springs, for early farmer L.H. Clay. The original Grasmere is the Lake District village in England that was home to poet William Wordsworth; there is still a Grasmere Drive in Apopka, near Wekiwa Springs. (Historical Society of Central Florida, Incorporated.)

Orlando's favorite early-aviation pioneer, Carl Kuhl, thrilled hometown crowds at the Central Florida Exposition in 1917. A teacher as well as a flier, he trained many pilots in both World Wars. (Historical Society of Central Florida, Incorporated.)

Organized in 1892, the Orlando Bicycle Club was a focus for the ladies, gents, and children who enjoyed a spin on the race track at Lake Eola or on paths through the woods, including one that led to the polo grounds near present-day Harry P. Leu Gardens. (Historical Society of Central Florida, Incorporated.)

Waiters at the deluxe Seminole Hotel in Winter Park, a few miles from downtown Orlando, pose for an undated photo. Known for its fine cuisine and hotel orchestra, the Seminole was a destination resort for many well-heeled Northerners. (Historical Society of Central Florida, Incorporated.)

On January 13 and 14, 1914, Orlando's Grand Theatre was the scene of a screening of Romance in Orlando, *filmed in the city the year before. The silent action picture featured members of the Orlando fire department and the palatial Braxton Beacham home on Orange Avenue. Jenkins Dolive played the young man who rescues his sweetheart, Mary Rock, from fiery doom. (Historical Society of Central Florida, Incorporated.)*

Founded by pharmacist James McElroy, who arrived in Orlando from Tennessee in 1881, the Blue Drug Store at 119 S. Orange Avenue was an Orlando institution for 60 years. "You Get What You Want," read its slogan in the city's 1907 business directory. On the east side of Orange between Pine and Church Streets, the drugstore was the most popular meeting place in town for Orlando's younger set because of its hospitality and legendary homemade ice cream, churned by hand in the back room of the store. (Historical Society of Central Florida, Incorporated.)

These boaters have no doubt embarked from the large boathouse behind them on Winter Park's Lake Osceola, near the site where the grand Seminole Hotel once stood. The first incarnation of the hotel opened on January 1, 1896. (Historical Society of Central Florida, Incorporated.)

July Perry was a 50-year-old church deacon, father, landowner, and labor contractor in the west Orange County community of Ocoee when he became the most well-known victim of far-reaching violence on the night of election day 1920 and the days following. Perry was lynched in Orlando and is buried in Orlando's Greenwood Cemetery.

Orlando's downtown bustled in the late 1920s, as this view looking north on Orange Avenue from Pine Street shows. The 1886 frame building that had housed the Dickson & Ives department store had been torn down in 1920 to make way for the four-story brick building (left) that still stands, housing offices. The Yowell-Drew building ("Quality Did It") faces it at right. (Historical Society of Central Florida, Incorporated.)

The intersection of Orange Avenue and Central Boulevard bustled during Orlando's boom times in the mid-1920s. The building with the clock at 1 North Orange Avenue, which originally housed the State Bank and Trust Company, was completed in 1924. (Historical Society of Central Florida, Incorporated.)

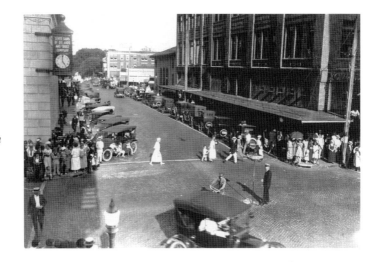

The Orange Court Hotel on North Orange Avenue made the cover of the Orlando Chamber of Commerce's slim magazine touting the city's charms in 1924. "Absorbingly interesting is Florida in the making," the copy declared. In Orlando, "you may wear the same clothes you would on Fifth Avenue" in New York, "and see the same sort of people."

Carl Dann's golf and country club at the old Apopka Road (now Edgewater Drive) and Par Avenue was built in 1924. Dann named it Dubstread to advertise that it was a challenging course dreaded by "dubs," or novice players. It is now owned by the city of Orlando. (Historical Society of Central Florida, Incorporated.)

"Mr. Cabco" appeared often in Orlando ads in the 1920s, as the symbol of the Cooper-Atha-Barr Company, developers of Orlando's College Park neighborhood. College Park's bungalows were built for "the common man," according to one story, "because there are so many of them." (Courtesy of Rick Kilby, KilbyCreative.)

Congregation Ohev Shalom built a neoclassical revival temple in 1926 at 525 East Church Street. George Miller, a son-in-law of settler Israel Shader, was the architect. In 1932, students at the temple school posed for this photo. The building was on Florida's Jewish Heritage Trail until its demolition in 2002. (Florida Photographic Collection.)

Fishing in Florida has long been a popular sport for women as well as men. This stylishly coiffed woman in the late 1920s or early 1930s might be at Lake Apopka near Orlando, the state's second-largest lake and long a fishing mecca until it became polluted by agricultural runoff in the late twentieth century. Massive efforts continue to reclaim the great lake. (Historical Society of Central Florida, Incorporated.)

The Albertson Public Library, precursor to the Orlando Public Library, formally opened on November 8, 1923. This view is likely from the 1950s. The architect, Murry King, also designed the 1927 courthouse a block west on Central Boulevard that now houses the Orange County Regional History Center.

Retired baseball great Joe Tinker, here with his wife Mary, arrived in Orlando in 1920 to manage the Orlando Tigers and stayed to become a well-known businessman. Tinker became a Hall of Famer in 1946. He died in Orlando on July 27, 1948, his 68th birthday. (Historical Society of Central Florida, Incorporated.)

Prohibition was a fact of life in 1920s Orlando as it was with the rest of the country. In 1926, Sheriff Frank Karel, with members of the Orange County Sheriff's Department and helpers, showed off the results of a still raid. The deputy at right in bow tie and hat, Dave Starr, would later become an Orange County institution as sheriff from 1949 to 1971. (Historical Society of Central Florida, Incorporated.)

Orlandoans were thrilled in 1936 to see hometown boy Buddy Ebsen dance with Shirley Temple in the movie Captain January, *just 10 years after Ebsen graduated from Orlando High in 1926. Ebsen was one of the best football guards in the school's history, yearbook editors wrote. In the 1920s, his father, Christian, founded a dance studio that would train generations in the city. (Historical Society of Central Florida,*

Floridians and visitors love to photograph themselves with alligators, dead or alive (although the latter definitely isn't advisable). This shot of an impressive specimen, likely from the 1920s, was found in an album belonging to Dr. V.L. Strayer of Orlando. Despite their lethargic appearance, Florida's trademark beasts can be lethal; always give them a wide berth. (Historical Society of Central Florida, Incorporated.)

Shoppers crowd near the cosmetics counter of the refurbished Yowell-Drew department store in 1926 to hear a lecture on "Proper Care of the Complexion." This may be the day in April 1926 when the store debuted a tea room on the mezzanine. One of the young women who worked there in the 1920s, Mickey Ekdahl, would become Orlando's Miss America in 1930. (Historical Society of Central Florida, Incorporated.)

Orlandoans turned out in force on January 11, 1927, for opening ceremonies at the new Atlantic Coast Line Depot at Sligh Boulevard, near Orlando General Hospital (now Orlando Regional Medical Center). The railroad's architect drew inspiration from the Spanish colonial missions in Santa Barbara and other California cities. (Historical Society of Central Florida, Incorporated.)

A grocery in the 1930s displays a sale of canned orange juice made by Orlando's own Dr. Phillips. His innovations and marketing efforts helped link orange juice with good health in American popular culture. (Historical Society of Central Florida, Incorporated.)

The citrus empire of Orlando's Dr. Phillips included a fruit-shipping plant at Dr. Phillips Landing near Sand Lake that was the world's largest when he opened it in 1928. Many of the workers in citrus packing plants were women. (Historical Society of Central Florida, Incorporated.)

These crowds on Orlando's Orange Avenue are likely celebrating the opening of the refurbished Yowell-Drew department store in 1926. Encouraged by the transformation of the Dickson & Ives store across the street, Yowell-Drew began a $150,000 remodeling in June of 1925 that included a central entrance on Orange Avenue with revolving doors. The Yowell-Drew store (later Ivey's) was on the southeast corner of Orange and Central; Dickson & Ives was on the southwest. (Historical Society of Central Florida, Incorporated.)

Swedish-born Margaret "Mickey" Ekdahl was a beautiful young woman (left and opposite page), according to Orlandoans who remember her from days she worked in both of the city's two major department stores. Crowned America's Sweetheart of 1930, she died after surgery in Orlando in 1932.

Miss America Is Dead

Miss Margaret Ekdahl, popular Orlando girl who won the title of Miss America in 1930, who died this morning.

FLORIDA'S FOR ROOSEVELT, SAYS PETER O. KNIGHT

NEW YORK, (Spl.) — Florida says Col. Peter O. Knight, Tampa attorney, financier and political boss will vote for Franklin D. Roosevelt, democratic nominee and "a repetition of its performance in 1928 is beyond all possibility."

Col. Knight said the democratic party is assured of victory if prohibition repeal is made the principal issue.

Knight

★ ★ ★ ★
BEAUTY AWARD WINNER DIES

Miss Margaret Ekdahl Is Victim of Sudden Peritonitis Attack

Miss America is dead.

Miss Margaret Ekdahl, 20-year-old blond beauty, who came to America from Sweden as a child and who at the age of 18 rose to national prominence by winning the Miss America national beauty award, died at 7:10 a. m. Thursday at the Orange General hospital.

Death followed an emergency operation for peritonitis, performed

---

Left column fragments:

IAY
USE
NTS

Gave
wer
ges

ISSUE

Stop
ew

Contro-
water-
d likely
t of at
Roose-
sidency.
mmuni-
Roose-
rity of
federal
on the
uilty of
d New

chair-
of New
r's tele-
July 10
which it
d with
of the
ng that
otiaions

g Mr.
a con-
York
o clear
ties be-
d into,
hat the
s had
y three

ld Mr.
int out
e state-
and the

r"
mmuni-
t smil-
ent let-
overnor
or con-
inistra-
seaway

UDIED

ight by

W. H.
e Bank
estab-

Orlandoans have always loved parades, a passion that could be indulged almost year-round. This 1930s event might be the children's Christmas parade to see Santa at the fairgrounds in 1932 or a similar promenade on Orange Avenue. (Historical Society of Central Florida, Incorporated.)

In 1932 architect James Gamble Rogers II built this home at 656 Interlachen Avenue in Winter Park for Robert Bruce Barbour using bricks from an earlier landmark, the 1886 Orlando Armory. Known as Casa Feliz, the house became a local cause celebre in 2001 when it was saved from destruction and moved to a new location on Winter Park's Park Avenue.

Leon Kazanzas (in the apron) readies a shipment of fresh citrus to go north by rail in 1937. Kazanzas's business, "Leon the Fruit Man," was long a fixture at 107 N. Orange Avenue in Orlando. Kazanzas would arrange for visitors to the nearby downtown hotels to ship fresh citrus to their homes or to friends in the North. The enterprise also included a small bar with cozy booths and the first slot machines in Orlando, Leon's son Jack Kazanzas says. The little boy is Jack's brother Leon Jr.; the man in the hat is the Railway Express agent; and Leon Jr. and Jack's half-brother, Henry Yelverton, is at far right. (Historical Society of Central Florida, Incorporated.)

In December 1947, Santa gets a hand from young Lewis and Stanley Yates on the front porch of the wooden post office at Christmas, Florida— a small historic community east of Orlando. Juanita Tucker, Christmas postmaster for more than 40 years, did much to develop the fame of the community's postmark and its reputation as a year-round haven for the holiday spirit. (Florida Photographic Collection.)

Businessman Harry P. Leu and his wife, Mary Jane, show off the results of a fine day's fishing, probably in 1932. Long a bachelor, Leu so surprised Orlandoans when he married the former Mary Jane Schnidli that the news made the front page of the Morning Sentinel *on September 8, 1932. (Courtesy of Leu House archives.)*

The roots of Central Florida cattle ranching go back to the area's earliest days of settlement, in the mid-1800s. Florida did not require fences around cattle lands until 1949, and the animals roamed freely. In addition to cattle and citrus, the ornamental-plant, vegetable, poultry, and dairy industries have also been important in Orange County's past. (Historical Society of Central Florida, Incorporated.)

On May 30, 1935, Orlando photographer Robert Dittrich snapped members of the Benevolent Protective Order of Elks 1079 at their Lodge at 409 East Central Boulevard, as they greeted members on a goodwill tour. A decade later, a committee of the Elks led to the founding of Orlando's Tangerine Bowl Commission and the city's first bowl game. (Courtesy of Andy Serros.)

Originally called the Research Studio, the Maitland Art Center was one of only three art galleries in Florida when it opened in 1938. The creation of artist and designer Andre Smith, its mix of Aztec, Mayan, and art deco styles has earned it recognition as one of America's most important examples of Fantastic architecture. (Courtesy of Maitland Art Center)

In the 1930s, when a telephone call involved only four numbers, Orlandoans could order groceries to be delivered from Joe's Fish & Poultry Market at 316 West Washington Street, owned by the Des Parois Brothers, Incorporated. (Historical Society of Central Florida, Incorporated.)

Soldiers parade on Orlando's Orange Avenue just north of the Central Boulevard intersection during an Army Day parade in 1942. Note the "quiet" sign on the San Juan Hotel. During the war, a giant siren was placed on the Orlando Utilities' building on Lake Ivanhoe; it could be heard for a radius of 18 miles. (Historical Society of Central Florida, Incorporated.)

In 1943, military officers and their dates take to the dance floor at Bill Kemp's Coliseum on Orlando's North Orange Avenue. A popular venue for dances and roller skating, the building boasted a 36-foot-high ceiling, supported by curved trusses that allowed for dancing and stage viewing unobstructed by support columns. (Historical Society of Central Florida, Incorporated.)

The community of Orlo Vista, west of downtown Orlando, hosted an annual cockfighting tournament that constituted the world series of the underground sport when this photo was snapped at the Orlo Vista pit in the late 1940s. At the time, cockfighting was not illegal in Florida, but betting on the fights was. (Historical Society of Central Florida, Incorporated.)

Central Florida underworld kingpin Harlan Blackburn (far left) was photographed partying with associates in a Polk County night spot in the 1950s. Blackburn ruled the syndicate that controlled the illegal numbers game called bolita in both Polk and Orange Counties. "He was the last of the old-style [Florida] mob guys," a retired law officer said when Blackburn died in prison in 1998. (Florida Photographic Collection.)

The Sanford-Orlando Kennel Club was a popular spot for legal wagering on greyhound races in Central Florida's booming post–World War II years. (The track continues in business in the twenty-first century.) Programs could be purchased at a variety of Orlando locales, including the Avalon Tap Room, the Angebilt Hotel Cigar Stand, and the Green Tree Grill at 371 N. Orange Avenue.

Gary's Duck Inn, at 3374 S. Orange Blossom Trail, opened in 1945 and became a landmark for locals and travelers alike. "We were here last night," a visitor wrote on the back of this postcard, mailed to New Hampshire in 1956. "Jo had the shrimp platter. I had deep-sea scallops, shrimp & tartar sauce with french fries. . . . . Very popular place. Crowded."

Windows are open in the days before air-conditioning in offices above the Lerner Shop, next to the Yowell-Drew department store, in this photo of Orlando's Orange Avenue from the late 1920s or early 1930s. Sam Y. Way, whose name is on the building above the shop, was mayor of Orlando in 1932–1934 and 1937–1940. (Historical Society of Central Florida, Incorporated.)

This photo of Orlando's most memorable motel, the vanished Wigwam Village at 700 S. Orange Blossom Trail, was taken in 1956. In its heyday in the 1940s and 1950s, the Village was recommended by travel mavens including Duncan Hines and boasted a grill, auto service, and a gift shop. The wigwams were torn down in 1973. (Florida Photographic Collection.)

Seen in a Robert Dittrich photo from the 1930s or early 1940s, Morrison's Cafeteria was long a downtown Orlando institution on West Central, just around the corner from Orange. Diners chose their own dishes and placed them on a tray, which was carried to their table by a waiter in a crisp white jacket. (Historical Society of Central Florida, Incorporated.)

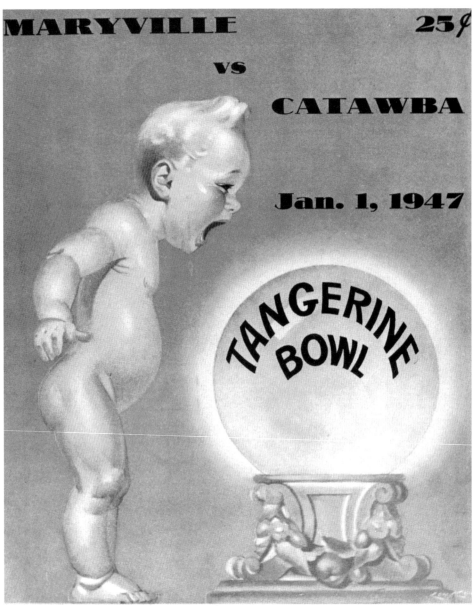

MARYVILLE   25¢

vs

CATAWBA

Jan. 1, 1947

Greater Orlando Stadium
Sponsored by ORLANDO LODGE 1079, B. P. O. ELKS

Orlando's first bowl game grew out of meetings at the home of Elks' treasurer Nick Serros, as the Orlando Elks Lodge sought a way to raise badly needed funds for their state project, a home for disabled children in Umatilla. About 9,000 people came out to see Catawba beat Maryville, 31–6, for the first Tangerine Bowl on New Year's Day 1947. "There had been a rodeo at the stadium for a week or so prior to the game," an attendee wrote years later. "Man, there was more white sand on the playing field for the game than there was at Daytona Beach." (Courtesy of Catawba College.)

Orange County grove workers gather their crop in this undated photo, perhaps from the 1930s or 1940s. The citrus workers were almost exclusively black men. In the late 1930s, when Zora Neale Hurston returned to Eatonville during her work for the Federal Writers' Project, she interviewed some of them, including John C. Hamilton, known by the nickname of "Seaboard" and reputed to be the fastest picker in Florida. The cutters were paid by the two-bushel box, 6¢ a box in the 1930s. The cutters were hired by the packing house, Hurston wrote, and were transported from grove to grove, sometimes riding distances of 75 miles to get to their work.

The Orlando area's first major tourist attraction, Gatorland and its toothy gate welcome visitors in a 1950s view. Unlike many vintage Florida attractions, Gatorland has managed to stay competitive in Central Florida's world of theme parks. Longtime residents like to take visitors there for a taste of old-style Florida.

Elvis Presley was 21 years old and America's biggest sensation when Orlando Sentinel *reporter Jean Yothers coaxed a kiss from him for the cameras during a backstage interview when he breezed through the city for two shows in a sweltering Orlando Municipal Auditorium on August 8, 1956. (Courtesy of Jean Yothers.)*

The large star decoration that has become traditional during December at Orange Avenue and Central Boulevard in Orlando began in 1955, according to research by Peggy Reed Mann, daughter of Dickson & Ives' owner Wilson Reed. He had bought the venerable department store on the southwest corner of the intersection in 1949 and wanted to do something special for the holiday shopping season, Mann says. This view is from the late 1950s.

Jack Kerouac was transformed from a struggling writer to a best-selling author during the months he lived in Orlando's College Park neighborhood, when **On the Road** *was published in the fall of 1957. The oak tree in the photo still stands by his College Park digs at 1418 Clauser Street, now owned by The Kerouac Project of Orlando. Kerouac wrote his novel* The Dharma Bums *in Orlando.*

THE ORLANDO FOUNTAIN
LAKE EOLA, ORLANDO, FLORIDA
1956

The illuminated fountain in Orlando's Lake Eola, an icon of the downtown landscape, almost eclipsed excitement in the skies when it was officially unveiled October 5, 1957, during Orlando's centennial celebration. The Soviet Union launched the satellite Sputnik on October 4. Planners of the fountain released this architects' rendering in 1956.

Central Floridians rushed outside to look at the eastern skies and cheer on May 5, 1961, when Alan Shepard became America's first man in space, flying a suborbital trajectory on a Mercury-Redstone vehicle. The launch pads at Cape Canaveral are about 50 miles east of Orlando on Florida's Atlantic Coast. (Florida Photographic Collection.)

Sales representatives for Tupperware Home Parties Incorporated pose in "spacettes" costumes during the company's 1960 jubilee for top sales personnel in the eastern United States. The company is based in Orlando. Inventor Earl Tupper's plastic products debuted in 1946, and in 1948 Tupperware began selling its wares in home parties that became a fixture of 1950s American culture. (Florida Photographic Collection.)

Colonial Plaza Shopping Center, seen in a late 1950s or early 1960s postcard, was the site of an all-day celebration when it opened on January 31, 1956. Stores on opening day included Belk's department store, where Orlando's first store escalator caused a sensation. Near Belk's, Ronnie's restaurant was long a fixture at the west end of Colonial Plaza's first section, facing Colonial Drive.

Orlando's downtown retail area was going strong in the late 1950s, when people came into the city from an area encompassing several counties to shop. In addition to Ivey's and Dickson & Ives at Orange and Central, major stores on Orange Avenue included Sears and J.C. Penney's, along with large "five-and-tens" including Kress, Woolworth's, McCrory's, and W.T. Grant. Specialty retailers included Gibbs-Louis women's store, Rutland's and Walter Menges' men's stores, the Youth Center for children, Brenner's for prom dresses, and many others. (Historical Society of Central Florida, Incorporated.)

Accompanied by Orlando Sentinel *publisher Martin Andersen (right), President Lyndon Johnson makes a campaign stop in Orlando in October 1964. The president arrived by plane at McCoy Jetport on Sunday, October 24, stayed at the Cherry Plaza Hotel, and later rode in a motorcade north on Orange Avenue and east to Colonial Plaza. More than 110,000 people crowded the route.*

Legendary American architect Frank Lloyd Wright was photographed with his student Nils Schweizer in the early 1950s, when Wright was inspecting the progress on his buildings at Florida Southern College in Lakeland, built under Schweizer's supervision. (Florida Photographic Collection.)

This image from the Florida Photographic Collection shows the Orlando Public Library about 1965. Nationally known architect John M. Johansen's monolithic structure likely remains one of Orlando's most controversial and most distinguished buildings. In the 1980s the library was expanded west to fill the whole city block under the guidance of Schweizer Incorporated, the firm led by Orlando-area Nils Schweizer, one of Frank Lloyd Wright's last students. The library "recalls an ancient fortress or cathedral with its tower-like structures housing elevators and stairways, with with its balconies, parapets and tall narrow windows," Clara Wendel wrote in a 1967 Library Journal *article. The poured concrete needed no cleaning, painting, or refinishing, Wendel wrote. "It actually improves with age, as the Florida sun bleaches it to a silvery warmth."*

Pedestrians head diagonally across an intersection in downtown Orlando in the 1950s. Although retailers and city leaders didn't know it at the time, the arrival of Colonial Plaza in 1956 and other malls that followed sounded the death knell for downtown Orlando's retail district. In the early twenty-first century, downtown has once more become home to offices and entertainment venues, but city planners are still working on a retail revival.

Hurricane season has long been a subject of concern and attention each year in Central Florida, although the Orlando area has been spared the devastation of the worst storms such as Andrew and the deadly hurricanes of 1928 and 1935. Hurricanes began getting names in 1950. This Orlando photo is from a destructive no-name storm in the late 1940s. (Historical Society of Central Florida, Incorporated.)

Now a major Central Florida cultural event each spring, the Winter Park Sidewalk Art Festival began officially in 1960, after an informal clothesline exhibit of work by artists and students in 1959. This view on Winter Park's Park Avenue was photographed in 1970. The juried festival draws thousands each March. (Florida Photographic Collection.)

Land that would become one of the most visited places on earth was untouched Florida wilderness about 1965 when representatives of the Walt Disney Company took a boating tour to inspect the future site of Walt Disney World. (Florida Photographic Collection.)

On Monday, November 15, 1965, Walt Disney, his brother Roy Disney, and Florida's Governor Haydon Burns flew into Orlando for two press conferences to announce news that would change Florida tourism forever. "Advance information is that it will not be a tinsel and gingerbread type of attraction," the Orlando Sentinel reported in Monday's paper. (Florida Photographic Collection.)

Complete Disney World Story In Section C

Orlando Sentinel

'Tis a Privilege to Live in Central Florida

Orlando, Florida, Friday, February 3, 1967

Florida's Disney World Unveiled: 'Supercalifragilisticexpialidocious'

50,000 New Jobs Due In 10 Years

By DON RIDER

Commercial, International Shopping Area, 50 Acres Of City Streets And Buildings
Rendering Shows EPCOT's Theme Hotel, Other Office Buildings Projecting Skyward Through Roof Of City

Impact Of Disney World

Sentinel Star Combined Daily Net Paid Circulation

Gain Over Last Year ... 4,920

Cracker Jim Sez

Today's Weather

The Orlando Sentinel *ran what may be the longest word ever to appear in one of its headlines on February 3, 1967, when it used "Supercalifragilisticexpialidocious" (from the popular 1964 Disney movie* Mary Poppins*) on its front page over a story about the coming Walt Disney World theme park. Sadly Walt Disney himself didn't live to see the outcome of his "Florida Project." He died of cancer on December 15, 1966.*

Selected as an astronaut in 1962, 1948 Orlando High School graduate John W. Young remains one of the city's favorite hometown heroes. Young is the first person to fly in space six times from Earth—seven times counting his lunar liftoff—according to the National Aeronautics and Space Administration (NASA). A historic marker sits in the front yard of Young's boyhood home at 815 West Princeton Avenue in College Park.

In 1974, Bob Snow (left) opened Rosie O'Grady's Good Time Emporium, and soon other eateries and shops followed at Snow's Church Street Station entertainment complex. Rosie's, a retro Gilded Age music hall, became the engine that pulled downtown Orlando from its early 1970s depths of desertion. A master showman, Snow promoted Rosie's with sky-writing and other aviation exploits featuring his friend Colonel Joe Kittinger (right), another Orlando legend and a member of the National Aviation Hall of Fame. In 1960, Kittinger executed the highest-ever parachute jump and was also the first balloonist to cross the Atlantic Ocean in a solo flight from Maine to Italy in 1984.

Arthur "Pappy" Kennedy (back left), who in 1972 became Orlando's first African-American elected officeholder, was honored in 1993 with a community-service award. Other honorees were (front, from left) Hudie Stone, Mildred Carter, and N.Y. Nathiri. Next to Kennedy are Stephen Brooks and the Reverend Julia

Walt Disney's mother, Flora Call Disney (above, with Walt), and his father were married on January 1, 1888, about 45 miles north of Orlando in Lake County, Florida. The couple's oldest son, Herbert, was born in Florida about a year later. Flora's sister Jessie Call Perkins and her husband, Albert Perkins, were longtime residents of Lake County. She taught school and eventually was principal of Eustis High School. Albert was postmaster of Paisley from 1902 until 1935. Jessie succeeded him after his death and served as postmaster until 1946. (Courtesy of The Walt Disney Company.)

Innovators, Artists, Cowboys, and Soldiers

Continued from page 64

Casa Feliz was the kind of structure residents assumed would sit there by Lake Osceola pretty darn near forever, barring hurricanes, fires, or sinkholes—the main disaster scenarios for Florida homeowners. But almost 70 years after Rogers built it, Casa Feliz became the center of a historic-preservation firestorm when destruction threatened it from a source that would likely amaze the wealthy Robert Bruce Barbour if he were alive today. A new owner aimed to tear down Casa Feliz to make way for something larger.

Somehow, after plenty of money-raising and placard-waving, Rogers' masterpiece survived. Casa Feliz became a Central Florida celebrity in the fall of 2001, as all 750 tons of it inched from its original site at 656 Interlachen Avenue across part of the Winter Park golf course. People came to stare and buy Casa Feliz tee-shirts as they watched the old armory brick walls ride their gargantuan chariot of steel beams and rubber tires, looking, as Gamble Rogers intended, like something far older than 1932, like something from a storybook. Casa Feliz is now settled comfortably on Winter Park's main street, Park Avenue, where it houses offices including those of the Winter Park Historical Association.

Not far from where Gamble Rogers left his legacy in bricks and stone, another visionary created his own architectural and artistic legacy in the Orlando area in the 1930s. The buildings Jules Andre Smith developed in Maitland also constitute one of Florida's architectural treasures. He called the place Espero, or Hope. "He wanted to be surrounded by people who were artists like he was," Central Florida artist Hal McIntosh said of Smith years later. "That's typical of an artist, wanting to create his own world."

An injury in World War I caused Smith's right leg to be amputated in 1924, a loss that added to his reclusive bent. He became a winter resident of Maitland in the early 1930s. Through Annie Russell, actress and professor of theater at Rollins College, he met Mary Curtis Bok, who would become the patron of his dream to create in Maitland an artists' colony—what he called the Research Studio, signified by the "RS" still above the front door of the art center today. When it officially opened on New Year's Day of 1938, the Research Studio was one of only three art galleries in Florida.

Eventually Smith's enclave encompassed three acres of natural gardens and 22 small buildings designed to nurture and inspire artists and visitors. Today, as the Maitland Art Center, it has a place on the National Register of Historic Places and has been called one of the most important examples of Fantastic architecture in America. The hundreds of carvings that adorn the buildings—stylized flowers, Aztec deities, suns, animals, angels—sprang from the imagination of a man who pondered other worlds than the present, physical one.

Stories have long persisted that Smith loved the haven he built for art in Florida so much he never left, and the Maitland Art Center's reputation as a window to the Other Side is chronicled in books such as Joyce Elson Moore's *Haunt Hunter's Guide to Florida* (1998). Of many Smith ghost stories, none beats what happened to the distinguished Central Florida artist William Orr one night in 1961.

In the late 1950s, Orr had shared a Winter Park studio with another painter, Robert Anderson, who had an unusual bond with Smith. Each had lost a leg to warfare: Smith in World War I, and Anderson in World War II. Smith was in the habit of paying an occasional visit to the Winter Park studio, and the two would share experiences. Because of the continued pain after his amputation, Smith rarely stood when Orr knew him, and he had never seen Smith walk. The two younger painters were thrilled when Smith offered them a show at his art center. They looked up to the older man; his death there in 1959 came as a shock.

About a year after Smith died, Orr had moved to a studio at the Maitland center. Now a single father with two young boys, he would sometimes go to the art center's main building at night to use the office phone to call his parents. The lights were off, but moonlight filtered in through a skylight. One night, his phone call over, Orr was heading toward the door when he felt the hair on the back of his neck stand up as he entered the central gallery. It felt like somebody's hand had passed up the back of his head. "I just stopped and froze," he recalls. Then, he turned, and in the dim light, "right there inside the door was Andre." The figure looked exactly as he had in life, except he was standing. "There was no fear involved at all," Orr recalls. "I stood there for about five minutes," Orr said, his eyes meeting Smith's. The spell was broken when the stunned Orr thought of his little boys and rushed to check on them through the front door, which closed and locked behind him. "What was that?" he remembers thinking.

In the months afterward, Orr completed the large portrait of Andre Smith that hangs in the entrance area of the art center. Over the years, stories of Smith's spectral activity continue to report a benign presence, says the art center's longtime executive director, James G. Shepp. Many of the artists who have studio space at the center feel Smith is still teaching them. It's "just as though there's someone there saying, 'Yes, that's right,' or 'Try it this way,' just the sort of little guidance they had felt from him," Shepp says.

In Smith's earthly role as mentor and artist, his works included scenes of life in nearby Eatonville as well as other black communities, and in the late 1930s he met and formed a friendship with the woman who would become the pride of Eatonville and the most famous daughter of the Orlando area, Zora Neale Hurston. She too was an artist, but one who used words rather than paint to form her lasting images of Florida life. Each year at the annual Zora Neale Hurston Festival of the Arts and Humanities, tens of thousands of people, from schoolchildren to luminaries of American letters, gather in her name in Eatonville, about 4 miles north of downtown Orlando.

About 100 years ago, Hurston was a schoolgirl in the little town herself, at what was then called the Robert Hungerford Normal and Industrial School. Founded in 1889 by Russell and Mary Calhoun, Hungerford was modeled on the famous Tuskegee Institute in Alabama, the Calhouns' alma mater. Hurston later recalled an incident about 1900, when white Northern educators visited the school. Charmed by the young Zora's out-loud reading of a Greek myth, the Northern ladies invited her to visit them at the Park House Hotel in Maitland, an exciting prospect for a child who, though nurtured by Eatonville, was already bursting to see the world that awaited outside. "They asked me if I loved school," she later wrote, "and I lied that I did." She did like some things about school, geography and reading, but she wasn't crazy about the "arrangement where the teacher could sit there" with a switch made from a palmetto and use it whenever he wished. "I hated things I couldn't do anything about, but I knew better than to bring that up right there, so I said, yes, I loved school."

It's a revealing vignette of a remarkable spirit, told in a Valerie Boyd's biography of the writer, *Wrapped in Rainbows: The Life of Zora Neale Hurston*. As Boyd makes clear, Hurston was not born in Eatonville, but in the small Alabama town of Notasulga, in 1891, which is a decade earlier than was long assumed to be the case. For Hurston, though, Eatonville was always home. "Essentially, everything that Zora Hurston would grow up to write, and to believe, had its genesis in Eatonville," biographer Boyd writes.

Zora's father, John Hurston, had learned of the town on a trip through Florida about 1890. In search of a place he and his family could thrive outside the stranglehold of the sharecropping system in Alabama, John Hurston was no doubt amazed when another traveler told him about an all-black town. "Not the black back-side of an average town," as Zora later wrote, but "a pure Negro town—charter, mayor, council, town marshal and all."

Eatonville was also a new town. One of the two or three first incorporated all-black municipalities in the nation, it got its official start August 15, 1887, at a meeting of 27 black men. Soon John Hurston would move his family there, to "the city of five lakes, three croquet courts, 300 brown skins, 300 good swimmers, plenty guavas, two schools and no jail-house," as Zora later described it. Her father, a charismatic preacher called "God's Battle-Ax," would later become a mayor of Eatonville.

Years later, after she was a published novelist, Zora returned to the town to take refuge and write in the late 1930s. She rented a big house on the edge of Eatonville, a former juke joint. Letters to friends in the North sent snapshots in words of her Florida. "I dislike cold weather and all of its kinfolk that takes in bare trees and a birdless morning," she wrote in one. In another, to her good friend Carl Van Vechten in 1938, she ended memorably:

> The orange trees are full of blossoms and I see you in every one of them. The
> bees are humming in the trees all day and the mocking birds sing all night in
> the moonlight. A wreath of flame vine for your crown, Zora.

She didn't have much when she died in Fort Pierce years later on January 28, 1960 and was buried in a segregated cemetery. Her grave was unmarked for years until the novelist Alice Walker made a pilgrimage to it in 1973, on a journey of discovery that fueled the renaissance of interest in Hurston and her literary reputation. On the marker, Walker chose an epitaph inspired by a poem by Jean Toomer: "Zora Neale Hurston: A Genius of the South."

In 1942, Hurston published a profile in the *Saturday Evening Post* that gave testament to the continued power of the cattle industry in the area settled by cattle drivers such as Aaron Jernigan a century before. In fact, the Florida Legislature did not require fences around cattle lands until 1949, when it passed a fencing law motivated in part by fears unwitting tourists would collide with cows ambling across the state's growing network of concrete roads.

Hurston's subject in the *Post*, Lawrence Silas, was the son of a man born into slavery. When she interviewed him in the early 1940s, he owned thousands of acres in Osceola County south of Orlando, more than 50 miles of fence, and thousands of cattle. Much of the land was along U.S. Highway 192, not far from the future site of Walt Disney World acreage that years later would breed shopping strips and subdivisions instead of fat cows sired by prize Brahma bulls.

The son of Tom Silas, who himself gained success raising Florida cattle, Lawrence Silas in the 1940s could look back on more than 40 years on the range. He was born in 1891. "Yeah, I've been fooling with cows and riding the swamps since I was five years old," he told Hurston. "I was so little, I had to let down the stirrup in order for me to reach it."

His knowledge of cattle and horses was legendary, and Hurston described his bank account as "chunky." He was wealthy as well in the respect of his peers and counted among his friends Florida beef barons such as the Lykes brothers, Tom and Howe. Silas lived until 1974, a self-made man who beat plenty of hardships, stampedes among them, to gain success and respect from his peers, white and black. Writing in the midst of World War II, Hurston declared, "He is important, because his story is a sign and symbol of the strength of the nation. . . . He speaks for free enterprise and personal initiative. That is America."

It took plenty of initiative to be a cattleman during the years of Florida's open range. "The horse was his transportation, and today's glamorized TV commercials of air-conditioned pickup trucks or helicopter roundups were not part of the 'cracker' cowboy's equipment," Henry Swanson notes in his history of Orange County agriculture.

Longtime east Orange County cattleman LaVerne Yates knows how tough it was. His granddad, John Burl Yates II, known as Bud, died in 1923 after he got sick on a cattle drive to Merritt Island, on the coast east of Orlando. Born in 1875, Bud Yates and his family would make trips from the Christmas area to Orlando about 1900 in a wagon pulled by oxen.

About 1940, Bud's then-teenage grandson LaVerne had his eye on some faster transportation, a pinto colt named Doby. "I paid $75 for him when he was about a year old," Yates recalls. It was a bundle; he could have bought a trained cow horse for $50, but he wanted that colt.

All the cowboys wanted him. Doby was the offspring of a Western mama, one of a couple of boxcar loads of horses that an owner of the Seminole Cattle Company had gone to Oklahoma to buy in the late 1930s. Money was likely even harder to come by in the Depression years in Oklahoma than in Florida, and the horses were a bargain. One of them was a mare that after her arrival in Florida gave birth to a genuine pinto—the only one on the Central Florida range, as far as LaVerne Yates knows. He worked hard, long days for a dollar a day to save for his goal. Doby wasn't big, and there were faster horses. But that pinto knew how to move.

That was important, both in work on the range, and in the informal races where cowboys cut loose for some weekend fun. They didn't just race horse against horse—they raced human against horse, for short sprints like 100 yards. At the drop of a handkerchief, the fellow on foot would take off, but the horse had to do a complete 360-degree pivot before it headed toward the finish line. If the horse took too many steps and took too long in the turn, it was the rider, not the runner, whose hopes of winning would stall at the starting line.

In one race on Christmas Cemetery Road, Yates and Doby were set up to race against Henry Barber, a fellow with a reputation for speedy feet. Cowpokes who had gathered for libations on Saturday night clamored into two cars to head over and see the action. The 100 yards were measured off, and the appointed judge, Edgar Bass, dropped the handkerchief. Yates turned his little horse around, and Doby hit the ground with his front feet and was gone like a shot. The race was his, but just barely. "I tell you what, man," Yates recalls, "if Doby had stumbled the least bit, Henry Barber would have outrun him."

Soon the cowboys' Saturday night races would end, as they traded their ponies for tanks and planes and marched off to war, LaVerne Yates among them. On the home front, the world of the Cracker cowboys and of everybody else in Central Florida would be changed forever by World War II, and the change would be greater, perhaps, than that wielded by any other event in the area's history.

"The greatest consequence of World War II for Florida was exposure," says historian Gary Mormino of the University of South Florida. "Florida was off the nation's radar screen" before the war, Mormino says. In 1945, after the war, Americans responding to a Gallup Poll listed Florida right behind California as the state to which they would most like to move.

During the war, many Americans got a look a Florida for the first time. The state's 1,200-mile coastline, expanses of palmetto prairie and pasture, and generally benign climate made it a magnet for military installations. Before the war, the state counted only eight bases; by 1945, it had 172, at least 10 that were in Central Florida. At Sanford Naval Air Station in Seminole County, more than half the pilots who would fight in the Pacific theater got their training not far from land on which Chief Coacoochee and his warriors had attacked U.S. soldiers a century before.

As the war loomed in 1940, the army added 740 acres to Orlando's municipal airport and transformed it into Orlando Army Air Base, and soon thousands of men in uniform poured in. After the war, the many who wanted to return and put down roots fueled a construction boom as well as a rise in population. Longtime Orlando builder Bill Demetree says:

> Think of all the men who came to train here. They came to Florida, they liked
> it and married girls. That was the first push of putting people in Florida, way
> before Disney or anything else. That's what spurred the growth.

The war years left indelible home-front memories. Betty Pfeiffer of Orlando remembers "going over to the beach and seeing lots of oil on the beach from where the tankers had been sunk" by German submarines. "There'd be sailors' shoes and clothes that had washed up. You couldn't help but be affected by that."

The best memories were of August 14, 1945, the day Orlando exploded in what one account called "the wildest celebration in all the city's long and colorful history." The war was finally over. On August 15, the front page of the *Orlando Sentinel* told the story: "Peace came to the world last night when President Truman announced that japan has accepted unconditional surrender and that Allied forces have been ordered to cease firing." The lack of a capital "j" on Japan was intentional. After Japanese forces attacked Pearl Harbor on December 7, 1941, *Sentinel* publisher Martin Andersen declared that all references to the enemy in his paper were not to be capitalized. He stuck to the style until the war's end, three years and more than eight months later.

In Orlando, the triumph was proclaimed noisily. Longtime Orlandoan Palmer Pierce remembers that he and his friend Keith Laube, both then about 13, joined the throng downtown. "My dad had a hand-cranked siren that put out a pretty good high-decibel level," Pierce recalls. The boys had gone to K.P. Pierce's tire-recapping business to pick up the siren, and they were cranking for all they were worth as they paraded on Orange Avenue, adding to the happy cacophony. "Louder, louder," people would holler at them as they passed. Celebrants ceremoniously burned "a token gallon of previously precious gasoline," the *Sentinel* reported, and screamed and tooted their automobile horns as they drove up and down "the Drag," as residents called Orange.

ORLANDO

At the Army Air Forces flight school and at Orlando Air Base, things were calmer. "All men living on the post were restricted to the reservation but found their way into small groups to listen to radio reports," one observer wrote, "and to pop the ever-present question, 'Wonder when I'll be getting out of the army?'"

As they wondered and looked ahead to life in the world after the war, many of them dreamed, too, of life under blue skies, where breezes rustled the oaks and they might fish on lakes that didn't freeze in winter. Now that the world was again at peace, it might be time to pursue those dreams, in Orlando.

Chapter Eight

FUN AND FANTASY IN THE SUN

The years after World War II saw Orlando's transformation from small "City Beautiful" to tourist-magnet metropolis in the making. In the 1940s, Orange County's population increased from about 70,000 to 114,000, and by 1960 it had more than tripled, to about 263,500. In the same two decades, the four counties of the metropolitan Orlando area (Orange, Osceola, Seminole, and Lake) also tripled, from almost 130,000 in 1940 to almost 395,000 in 1960. (By 2000, the four-county area counted more than 1.6 million.)

It was after the war, too, that Florida's role as a retirement haven really took off. The New Deal had transformed the reality of growing older in America. Armed with portable Social Security benefits and hearty union pensions, many Americans enjoyed a new flexibility in retirement that enabled them to ride the wave of postwar optimism south to the sun. Postwar guidebooks to Florida retirement brimmed with can-do brio. Some, such as George and Jane Dusenbury's *How to Retire to Florida*, offered useful tips; others relied more on enthusiasm than practicality. Filled with testimonials of rich golden years fueled by fresh orange juice, books such as William H. Bates's *You Can Live Longer in Florida* offered the prospect of not only a better life, but an extended one. "If they lived back North," Bates wrote, these revitalized new Floridians would be "laid up with rheumatism or otherwise incapacitated, if they had not completely passed out of existence. They seem to go on forever in Florida."

The flood of retirees into the state indeed seemed as though it would go on forever as the century moved on. When the first Social Security checks were mailed in 1940, Florida had about 2,500 beneficiaries, similar to Delaware. But throughout the 40 years after 1950, 1,000 retirees poured into the state each week. The state's older-than-65 population skyrocketed by 70 percent during the 1970s and then by 40 percent more during the 1980s, representing an immense source of political clout and financial power.

In the years after the war, these older folks and many younger ones, too, took to the nation's burgeoning road system to try out a Florida vacation and perhaps put down roots. It was time to roll down the top on the convertible—maybe an aqua one with big fins in the 1950s. It was time to take to the highway and have some fun. Orlando was ready and waiting.

As the swinging 1940s looked forward to the rocking 1950s, one of the best places in town to have a good time was Bill Kemp's Coliseum on North Orange Avenue. Some folks called it "the working man's country club." Kemp didn't build the Coliseum, but he put it at center stage in Orlando in the 1940s and 1950s, after he bought it in 1937. For nearly 50 years, the big hall and its satellites, the Aquaseum swimming center and Bowliseum lanes, served as a focus of fun.

In 1948, New Year's Eve would cost a couple $2.90 each to put on their party hats and dance to the music of Art Mooney and his orchestra. Tommy Dorsey, Glenn Miller, Harry

ORLANDO

James, Guy Lombardo, Sammy Kaye, Gene Krupa—you name the band, and W.R. Kemp had booked them.

Early in the 1940s, Kemp's stepson Paul Pirkle had opened a grill and soda fountain right next to the Coliseum. Customers could munch on an egg and olive sandwich or a BLT for 15¢; on the high end, a 16-ounce T-bone dinner was $1.10. The house specialty, frosty milk shakes in chocolate, vanilla, or cherry would cost you a dime; if you wanted them "double rich," it was 15¢.

Built just before the Jazz Age land boom went bust in Central Florida, the Coliseum opened in December 1926. It boasted the city's first public swimming pool, an Olympic-sized excavation that was used rarely, if at all, until Kemp took it over. The pool had no dressing rooms or bathhouse; Kemp eventually added those to open the Aquaseum.

Inside his Coliseum, the solid maple dance floor was 114 feet wide and 132 feet long, 36 feet below a ceiling buttressed by giant curved trusses that eliminated the need for columns. The wide open space offered patrons a clear view of the bandstand and a great place to dance and rollerskate.

Born in Georgia about 1900, Bill Kemp had a law degree from Columbia University, but it was in sunny Florida where his genius really blossomed. He thrived on making things happen: on planning and promoting events. Generations of teenagers had their first big nights out at skating parties or dancing at the Coliseum, often on church outings. "It was a great thing for us," the late Joe D'Agostino Jr. told the *Orlando Sentinel* in 1971, after Kemp's death, as he remembered the Coliseum in the 1950s:

> The hall looked so big, and it was fixed up like a big ballroom. It was something
> we young kids never got to see anywhere else. There was really no place else to
> go in Orlando that could compare with it.

Eventually, the big bands faded, but the Coliseum continued as a skating rink and venue for rock concerts. And many youngsters spent summer afternoons by the Aquaseum pool, pumping coins into the jukebox when they weren't doing cannonballs off the diving board. After both Bill Kemp and his wife, Bessie, died in 1971, their children inherited the property and kept it going for a little while, but the building was badly damaged by fire in 1972 and subsequently torn down.

The teenagers who danced and skated at the Coliseum in the late 1940s and 1950s also looked forward to a special treat each year when Central Florida's big annual fair resumed in Orlando after the war. The first postwar fair was in 1946, and by 1947 things were in full swing. Exposition Park's first permanent livestock barn was completed that year, and the State Boys and Girls 4-H Clubs sent entries to their Poultry Show from all over Florida. At the American Legion exhibit, visitors could see Emperor Hirohito's white horse on display.

For many children and teens, the lure of the fair was the carnival midway. A school holiday would let students take advantage of free admission until noon and also reduced prices for the midway, where they might scare themselves silly on rides and also get a look at the snake house, glass house, fun house, "Iron Lung," and "Fat Girl."

The last two attractions were part of the sideshows displaying so-called human oddities (and animal oddities as well) that were a mainstay of European and American carnivals for many years. They are gone from most American carnival midways, and a cheery 1947 Orlando news story about the attractions once called "freak shows" seems shocking from the vantage point of post-2000 America. The sideshows were under the management of three brothers, the story said, who "spend their winter months hunting freaks," a pastime the men said was "as interesting and as exciting as big game hunting. They must follow all sorts of leads, which have carried them to all parts of the world."

For many years at annual fairs in Orlando, the midway was the province of a man whose name by the 1950s was synonymous with the Central Florida Exposition: James E. Strates. Strates had immigrated to Massachusetts from Greece in 1909 at the age of 15. He perfected his skills as a wrestler billed as "Young Strangler Lewis" while traveling the Northeastern carnival circuit before starting his own show in the early 1920s. Before his death in 1959, Strates had become an admired figure in Central Florida business as well as national carnival circles. He presided over a company that in the late 1950s traveled in 50 railroad cars and employed as many as 1,000 people. The Strates family still runs the Orlando-based Strates Show Incorporated, which provides amusement rides, games of skill, and food concessions to fairs and festivals along the Eastern Seaboard.

About the time the fair got going strong again after its wartime hiatus, Orlando found itself in the pages of *Time* in connection with another yearly event. A tournament of international renown was bringing tough champions from far and wide to the small Southern city, the magazine said in 1948.

These feisty competitors were backed by sporting men from all over the country, including a Texas oil millionaire, a Philadelphia income-tax lawyer, and a reputed professional gambler from Memphis. The Philadelphia man crowed to the *Time* writer that he trained his champs on a special diet that included "such highfalutin food as cakes with French brandy, oysters, apples, sprouted oats, plain oats, eggs and flint corn."

There was plenty of crowing going on, because the high-stakes contest was a gathering of what the *Time* writer called "the chicken men"—owners and trainers of gamecocks. "Come on, red rooster, kill him," one woman yelled from the crowd during a match. Fourteen chicken men had each posted $1,000 to enter what amounted to the World Series of cockfighting. It took place each year in Orlo Vista, just west of downtown Orlando.

The cockfighting pit was housed in "a barnlike structure with a seating capacity of more than 1,000," according to the 1939 Federal Writers' Project guidebook to Florida. The season, which ran from Thanksgiving until July 4, reached its apex in January with the international tournament sponsored by the Orlando Game Club. "Held regularly since 1920, the tournament has become in its field what the Kentucky Derby is to followers of the turf," the guidebook says. Some of the gamecocks arrived by private railroad cars. In 1948, the heaviest hitter among the chicken men was former boxer Bobby Manziel from Texas, who had struck it rich wildcatting for oil on $700 borrowed from his pal Jack Dempsey, according to *Time*. Manziel's birds arrived in a special plane.

And was this all legal? Well, sort of. The controversial, bloody sport of cockfighting was long legal in Florida; it was the betting on the birds that wasn't. But heavy betting indeed took place around the pit at Orlo Vista, and so secrecy veiled the matches. As *Time* described the scene, "The usual bet was $100. The big ones—$1,000 and up—were made more quietly, by a whisper, a nod, a flick of the finger. On the wall was a sign saying 'No profanity allowed.' There was none. In the audience, one woman fed a baby from a bottle."

The crowd was eclectic. Even Dr. Philip Phillips, the citrus king, was said to have enjoyed a visit or two to the local matches, and he surely wasn't alone among area luminaries. Other visitors came from far and wide. At the 1948 event, one of the most prolific chicken men was John Kehoe, a tough old Pennsylvania bird who cheered on his fighting fowl from his wheelchair. "I fight chickens, you know. I'm proud of it—keeps me alive," he bellowed to the *Time* reporter.

Just as bright sunshine produces spots of shade, it's not surprising that the Sunshine State had its quota of shady areas, including the Orlo Vista cockfights. In other areas of Florida life, folks walked even farther into the shadows. In 1950 and 1951, a United States Senate Crime Investigating Committee headed by Senator Estes Kefauver uncovered some of the darkest spots after months of investigation. The committee confirmed the existence of organized crime as a national network with roots deep into Florida, and provoked a flurry of law-enforcement activity, including attempts to deport crime kings.

Not all of the crime kings were foreign born, though. "Closely Knit Underworld Clamps Gambling Hold on Lethargic Central Florida" read a headline in the *Tampa Tribune* in July 1950. The story ran under the label "Bible Belt Bolita"—a reference to the lottery-style numbers game that had been imported from Cuba in the 1880s. In 1950, bolita was the bread and butter of underground Florida.

Central Florida, "where many of the very best people live," harbored "more than a fair share of gamblers and hoodlums," the *Tribune* stated. Folks by then had heard something about the power of Tampa's underworld, "but somehow one looks for better things in the beautiful citrus cities, their church spires reaching heavenward."

In no city did the spires reach higher than Orlando, where "some of the biggest numbers operators in Florida have holed up and are doing a multimillion-dollar business." In Central Florida cities, the bolita bigwig was usually "a local boy," the *Tribune* stated. In Orlando, he was Harlan Blackburn.

"He was kind of the last of the old-style mob guys," a retired law officer said at Blackburn's death in prison in 1998. "He had a reputation as someone you didn't mess with." He had friends you didn't mess with either, especially Santo Trafficante Jr., the reputed godfather of Florida. Blackburn wore a ring with a big diamond in it that looked exactly like one Trafficante wore. The story went that the rings had been made from earrings belonging to Trafficante's mother, but that's not true, Blackburn's one-time associate Clyde Lee told the *Orlando Sentinel* years later. "Blackburn was trying to copy Santo," Lee said, and he had a ring made to match the one Trafficante wore.

Known in his heyday as "the Colonel," Blackburn rose to wealth from poor beginnings as the son of an itinerant construction worker. He once claimed to have started his gambling businesses with $90,000 in black-market cash he made while serving as a military policeman in Europe during World War II. It's likely Blackburn hooked up with the Trafficantes—Santo Sr. and Santo Jr.—not long after the war and ran the Orlando-based bolita network with their blessing.

It's easy to forget, after years of cinematic glamorization of organized crime, that men like Blackburn were not the same as Marlon Brando with cotton in his cheeks. Clyde Lee, the man who knew about Blackburn's diamond ring, could tell you that. One morning in 1971, Blackburn phoned Lee and told him to go to a pay phone at State Road 434 and Interstate 4 in Seminole County. As Lee closed the door, a car roared by, and Lee was shot six times. He survived, and the man charged with the hit was acquitted, but Blackburn was convicted of aiding and abetting attempted murder. He was also convicted on federal tax and gambling charges and spent much of the rest of his life behind bars until his death in 1998.

In the 1950s, Orlandoans of every social stripe amused themselves by buying chances in the bolita numbers game that was run, behind the scenes, by Blackburn—now long made obsolete by the state's lottery—but they also pursued more wholesome pleasures on a Saturday night. If they or their tourist visitors wanted to dine out, they might head to the Orange Blossom Trail to a now-gone Orlando institution, Gary's Duck Inn, the restaurant that would later become the inspiration for the Red Lobster chain.

"Yum-Yum," exclaimed the 1954 edition of Duncan Hines's *Adventures in Good Eating* about Gary's. Hines's guide that year included just four eateries in Orlando. The others were downtown: Harry's on Orange Avenue, Markham's Hibiscus Room at the Eola Plaza, and Morrison's at the San Juan Hotel. To dine at Gary's, travelers heading south through town had only to make a quick right turn. The restaurant opened its doors at 3974 South Orange Blossom Trail in January 1945. It survived almost 50 years before closing in late 1994.

Like many American success stories, the landmark had humble beginnings. When Gary and Caroline Starling began it in 1945, they had three employees and seating for 15 patrons. By 1957, they employed 55 people. In 1945, they served customers 2,000 pounds of shrimp. By late 1957, "during the recent lobster season, customers consumed 85,000 pounds of the Florida delicacy," a newspaper story reported. That's a lot of lobster, but the image Gary's most often used to whet customers' appetites was a giant ring of gargantuan shrimp with a container of cocktail sauce plopped in the middle. Every day in the newspaper, the fried-shrimp platter appeared in Gary's ads, looking a little like a flying saucer made of seafood. With it was always the slogan "Where good food predominates."

In 1963, a group of investors bought Gary's. They included Charles Woodsby, the Darden brothers, Bill and Denham (restaurateurs from Waycross, Georgia), and Al Woods, who managed Gary's until the late 1970s. It was in Gary's, the story goes, that the four men decided a chain of similar, informal seafood eateries might be the recipe for even greater success. They opened the first Red Lobster in Lakeland in 1968 and by 1970 had expanded to five locations, which they sold that year to General Mills Incorporated. Today there are hundreds of Red Lobsters across the country.

The 1954 Duncan Hines guidebook mentions one other Gary's dish besides the famous shrimp platter: hush puppies, those little cornmeal bundles of fried delight. In *Cross Creek Cookery* (1942), Florida's great writer Marjorie Kinnan Rawlings declared hush puppies "in a class by themselves." "Fresh-caught fried fish without hush puppies are as man without woman, a beautiful woman without kindness, law without policemen," Rawlings wrote. The name, she said, honors the hungry pooches who howled until cooks tossed leftover bits of fried cornmeal batter to them, calling "Hush, puppies!" Devouring the warm morsels, the dogs "could ask no more of life," Rawlings said, "and hushed." Here, from a postcard, is Gary's recipe:

ORLANDO

HUSH PUPPIES

2 cups enriched white corn meal

1/3 cup flour

2 teaspoons baking powder

1 1/2 teaspoon salt

2/3 cup of ground Spanish onion and juice

2 tablespoons melted butter

1 egg

2/3 cup milk (more of less if needed, according to onion juice)

Sift meal, flour, baking powder and salt together. Add butter, onion and juice to dry ingredients. Add beaten egg. Add enough milk to make a soft dough. Drop by spoonfuls in deep fat at 375 or 400 degrees about four or five minutes.

The name for the road where travelers could duck in to Gary's restaurant was a stroke of marketing genius: Orange Blossom Trail. Not a road or a highway, like the Dixie Highway, but a trail, a word hinting of exploration, adventure, America's frontier spirit—and made of orange blossoms. During an Ohio or Michigan winter, the phrase could infuse the daydreams of a would-be road wanderer with visions of sweet fruit, sunny days, and fragrant nights. And in the 1940s and 1950s, boosters of Florida tourism applied it not only to a Central Florida route but also to a ribbon of roadway that brought travelers down the middle of the state, mostly on U.S. Highways 441 and 27. In late 1937, the Greater Orlando Chamber of Commerce had voted to change the name of Kentucky Avenue to the Orange Blossom Trail, and it's likely that not long afterward the Trail in Orlando gained what would be for many years its most distinctive landmark—the Wigwam Village Motel, a vanished treasure of roadside Americana.

Many Central Florida residents or visitors have a mental snapshot of those giant wigwams stashed somewhere in memory. They were not something you saw every day: 27 steel-and-stucco wigwams sat in an immense horseshoe with the open end facing the Trail. And at that end of the U-shaped village stood four more wigwams: a mother-ship teepee flanked by three small satellites in a constellation that probably housed the restaurant and manager's dwelling as well as the motel office. For generations raised on movie, television, and radio heroes such the Lone Ranger and Tonto, the big wigwams sang an irresistible siren song of a West that never was, except in imagination. When families in big, tail-finned cars sailed south down the Trail, the sounds of "Daddy, Daddy can't we stay *there*" were inevitable.

The motel stood until early 1973, when the *Orlando Sentinel* reported its demolition on February 15. Its origins are not as easily documented, but by the late 1940s it was clearly out there on the Trail, on the frontier not only of the city limits but also of America's burgeoning fascination with highway travel. Like some of the families who traveled south for Florida vacations, it had roots farther north, in Kentucky, where a man named Frank Redford opened a wigwam-style grill and gas station in 1931. By 1933, Redford had added 15 teepee-shaped cabins for travelers at Horse Cave, Kentucky, the first of seven related Wigwam Villages across America. In 1937, Redford patented his wigwam design featuring stucco walls over a steel frame, supposedly a fantasy translation of a Sioux village he had seen in South Dakota.

That same year he added Village Number 2, in nearby Cave City, Kentucky. Redford owned the pair in Kentucky; the other five, including the one in Orlando, Wigwam Village Number 4, were franchises. With 27 motel units compared with 15 at the Kentucky motels, Orlando's was likely the largest of the lot.

The Cave City village is on the National Register of Historic Places and is a designated historic landmark of the Kentucky Heritage Council. Another surviving, often-photographed Wigwam Village is on Old Route 66 in Holbrook, Arizona.

Not far from Orlando's Wigwam Village on the Orange Blossom Trail, locals and visitors could stay cool on summer evenings at a drive-in movie, a popular Florida pastime in the days before central air-conditioning took hold in the 1960s. Begun in the early 1930s in New Jersey, the outdoor theaters, or "ozoners," had taken a while to catch on, but by early 1942, film industry reports counted 95 of them in 27 states. Six of the 95 were in Florida, including the Orlando Drive-In Theater on South Orange Blossom Trail. By 1948, the national total had mushroomed to 820, and by 1958 it zoomed to a peak of about 4,000.

In Orlando, by the early 1950s the drive-in on the South Trail had plenty of competition. In July 1950, for example, the Winter Park Drive-In on U.S. Highway 17-92 was touting the "first Central Florida showing" of Roy Rogers and Dale Evans in *Trigger Jr.*, "Filmed in Beautiful Trucolor." At the Prairie Lake, Joan Crawford was emoting under the stars in *The Damned Don't Cry* (plus "Cartoons and the Latest News from Korea!"). At the Washington Shores Drive-In, advertised in those days of segregation as a "colored theatre," patrons were offered *Malaya* with James Stewart and Spencer Tracy. The Kuhl Avenue drive-in in south Orlando favored a Western for its first feature, as did the Ri-Mar on the North Trail. Later, in the 1960s, the screens would flicker with the likes of Vincent Price in the Hammer Films horror classics or reruns of that made-in-Florida classic *The Creature from the Black Lagoon* (1954).

But that would be later, when the theaters were turning more and more to a teen audience for survival. In 1950, the ozoners were still on the rise. Now, almost all in Florida are gone. The last holdouts in Orange County were the Ri-Mar in Lockhart, the victim of fire as well as declining audiences, and the Starlite in Winter Garden, which was still going strong until the late 1990s. Despite a strong volunteer "SOS" effort in 1996 to "Save Our Starlite," that last outdoor picture show vanished too from its West Plant Street location across from the VFW hall. "I've seen grown-ups before in their nightgowns," a young Starlite patron said. "They don't care. It's like a second home, I guess."

Indoor movies also offered havens for Orlandoans on warm days and nights. "Relax in cool comfort at Florida State Theatres," read the banner over five movie ads on a Saturday in 1951. The "COOL" is rendered in fat, round letters festooned with ice. The five theaters touted were, in Orlando, the Beacham, Rialto, Roxy, and Grand, and in Winter Park, the Colony. Ads for two other indoor theaters, the Lincoln and Carver, designated each a "Colored Theatre" in small type. The Vogue, at Mills, and Colonial served the Colonialtown neighborhood.

Of the bunch, the Grand was the oldest. On the north side of Pine Street just west of Orange Avenue, it had been one of Orlando's prime silent-movie palaces until businessman Braxton Beacham, also the city's mayor in 1907, built the grander Beacham on Orange Avenue in 1921, with a seating capacity of 1,200. "Located in the heart of the city, it is constructed entirely of concrete, and is fireproof," ads said. Built a few years too early for the high glory days of American movie palaces, the Beacham never had the eye-popping fantasy of the famous Fox theater in Atlanta or the Tampa Theatre, built in the west-coast Florida city in 1926. But it was for many years Orlando's premiere movie theater, complete with balcony, red curtain, and extravagantly flowered carpeting.

In 1955, when the Beacham was pulling crowds in with *The Tender Trap*, another Orlando institution got its start about a block away, at the corner of Orange Avenue and Central Boulevard. It's the big illuminated star that hangs at the intersection during the Christmas holiday season. In those years before the rise of shopping malls, most folks did their holiday shopping downtown. Orlandoan Wilson Reed had bought the venerable Dickson & Ives department store on the southwest corner of Central and Orange in 1949, and "he wanted to do something special downtown," his daughter Peggy Reed Mann remembers.

In 1955, Reed's store and Ivey's across the street joined forces to hang a giant star between them. The decoration sent the stores' "mutual good wishes" to Central Florida shoppers, a news item said. The two retail emporiums had long ruled at Orange and Central, dueling department stores in the tradition of Macy's and Gimbel's in the New York world of the vintage holiday movie *Miracle on 34th Street*. On the east side was Yowell-Drew-Ivey, formerly the Yowell-Drew Company, which had been on the site since 1917. Later it would become simply Ivey's. There you could find everything from the newest Nancy Drew book to the latest fashions. The store's elegant window displays were curtained on Saturday night, so patrons wouldn't be tempted even to window shop on Sunday. To the west across Orange Avenue was Dickson & Ives. Older Central Florida ladies still sigh with regret at the loss of its shoe department, beloved for the bounty and style of its offerings.

As shoppers in the 1950s bustled between the two stores at holiday time, pausing to take in their window displays full of red and green, the star hung overhead, suspended between the two brick stores from strings of bright lights. Orlandoans bonded with it while they scurried in search of gifts and also as they watched Orlando's big annual holiday parade.

"I can remember so clearly standing in the cool weather outside Ivey's in 1953 to watch the parade," longtime resident Jeanette Derry of Orlando says. "Either the Edgewater or Boone High School band led off the parade—I can't recall which one—and the other one marched at the end." For students marching down Orange Avenue on a chilly night—perhaps in a band from Edgewater, Boone, or Jones, the undisputed masters of marching style—that big star was ahead, telling you that you were almost there, almost at the thick of things where the crowds were heaviest and the excitement the most intense.

Started in the 1930s by *Orlando Sentinel* publisher Martin Andersen, the parade transformed and changed sponsors several times, and early in the 1990s faded away. Its big star vanished for a time but was reincarnated in a new 13-foot version in 1984, when a group of longtime Orlandoans helped raise $13,000 to revive the tradition. But, by 1998, that too seemed headed for the trash pile. The plexiglass was cracked, city officials said, and repair estimates for the star and some other venerable decorations had come in as high as $40,000.

Orlandoan Jack Kazanzas got busy. Kazanzas grew up in the Orlando, the child of parents who had a business in the city for 40 years. He knew the downtown star was a powerful symbol for longtime residents. In 1998, using glue and glass cleaner, he was able to get the star into shape for its annual appearance. In the next couple of holiday seasons, he and his ad hoc star committee had raised several thousand dollars for a complete refurbishment of the symbol of downtown Orlando's past. "I'm just trying to save an old tradition," Kazanzas said. "It just burns me up that everything has to be constantly changing."

But, in Orlando, "constantly changing" was becoming a way of life, the by-product of the area's by-now steady engine of growth. Central Florida had invited America to come on down, and the call was being answered. Orlando's own Carl Dann had predicted it, way back in the 1920s. As he looked back on the Jazz Age boom days in a memoir at the end of that decade, Dann forecast the area's future with uncanny accuracy.

> There is one simple reason why the future of Florida is an absolute fact, and that reason is this. If you go straight north from Central Florida, you will not go to New York City; you will go to Cleveland, Ohio. New York City is several hundred miles to the right; Chicago to the left. There is a great funnel, or V-shape, with Florida as the vertex. In this funnel, or V, resides the majority of the population of the United States. Sixty percent of them are only one night out.

By the 1950s, they were on the way.

Chapter Nine

ICONS AND ICONOCLASTS

As the 1950s moved into the 1960s, Orlando was changing with almost bewildering speed and intensity. It wasn't just the influx of tourists and new residents. The world was changing, and Central Florida found itself at the forefront of the space age. Orlando was the closest major city to the United States' new missile-test center at Cape Canaveral, the precursor to the Kennedy Space Center. The transformation of the Cape and the arrival soon after of the Martin Company to Orlando had an impact on the city equal to the land boom of the 1920s.

Within hours of the announcement in 1956 that the Martin Company, the builder of the Matador Missile, had purchased 10 square miles south of the city for a plant site, property values zoomed overnight in southwest Orlando, with some prices jumping from $200 to $1,000 an acre in a matter of hours.

Not only Orlandoans but all Americans had their eyes on the sky, especially in 1957. It was a big year for the City Beautiful. One hundred years earlier, Judge James Speer had engineered his picnic election in which soldiers had exchanged votes for a good meal and ensured that the settlement soon named Orlando would become the county seat, rather than Sanford or Apopka. Now, on the centennial of their city's official beginnings, Orlandoans got ready to celebrate. As they did, on an October morning, the whole world changed.

Up in West Virginia, a young Homer Hickam woke up that morning and stumbled downstairs to breakfast. Years later, he would write about it in his book *October Sky*. As he and his mother ate buttered toast and sipped hot chocolate to fend off the fall chill, Hickam heard a steady beep-beep-beep coming from the radio, from something the announcer called Sputnik. "Mom looked from the radio to me," Hickam says. " 'What is this thing, Sonny?' " He knew, exactly. It was a satellite. "It orbits around the world. Like the moon, only closer," he told his mom. "We were supposed to launch one this year, too. I can't believe the Russians beat us to it!"

Neither could the rest of America. "Russia Launches Earth Satellite—Radio Signals Believed Heard from 'Moon,' " read the front page of the *Orlando Sentinel* on October 5, 1957, the same morning Hickam heard the beeps on the radio. Sputnik had gone up October 4, the same day in history's record books that the television series *Leave It to Beaver* premiered on CBS.

It was an appropriate juxtaposition for the times: In the late 1950s and early 1960s, Americans and Orlandoans experienced a sometimes surreal blend of the serious and the wonderfully silly, the scary and the comforting, the familiar and the unknown. Sputnik certainly had its frightening aspects. With the launch of the "first earth satellite ever put in globe-girdling orbit under man's controls, the Soviet Union claimed a victory over the United States," the *Sentinel* said. That was serious business in Cold War days. Also serious was the news dominating headlines in the days around the Sputnik launch: the school integration crisis in Little Rock, Arkansas. On October 4, national guardsmen had broken up "a menacing throng of white students" at newly integrated Central High School. "Come on, you chickens, . . . Dirty chicken," white anti-integration demonstrators shouted at other white students who stayed inside the school. "For an ugly split-second it appeared a new riot might be building in the street before the school where blood was shed in adult riots and demonstrations last week," the *Sentinel*'s front page said.

But in Orlando the next day, October 5, as people kept one wary eye on the October sky and on the reports from Little Rock, they also marveled at an earthly wonder right there at home. "Russia may have its earth satellite, but Orlando for the last two days seems to have been more interested in its new Centennial fountain at Lake Eola," the *Sentinel* reported October 6. At twilight, thousands of people had circled the lake to see the fountain's spouting waters and changing colors. The fountain's debut was the centerpiece of a daylong 100-year birthday party, "the biggest, noisiest, longest celebration" in the city's history, the newspaper proclaimed.

After a parade, water-ski show, medicine-ball battle, tug of war, "judo demonstration," fashion show, model plane fly-in, and numerous band concerts, the highlight of the day had arrived when the fountain in Lake Eola, "a permanent monument to the city's first century, was turned on at 8 p.m.," the paper said. "The crowd gasped as the main spout shot water 75 feet into the air, the multi-hued lights came on, and smaller spouts around the fountain's rim threw a fountain of water around the beautiful edifice."

Especially proud was the fountain's chief champion, Linton Allen, board chairman of the city's First National Bank. During his post–World War II travels in Europe, Allen had seen impressive fountains in Europe's beautiful cities, and he got the idea for a new trademark for Orlando: an illuminated fountain in Lake Eola. In 1956, Allen had rounded up a group of civic leaders to help support his idea and had broached it to the Orlando Utilities Commission (OUC), which gave a thumbs-up.

Landscape architect William C. Pauley of Atlanta designed and engineered the plastic and concrete dome; Peninsula Construction built it on a cost-plus-fixed-fee contract with OUC, the *Sentinel* said. Pilings using 28 steel cylinders 60 feet long were driven into the lake bottom and filled with concrete. Then, 320 tons of concrete were carried by barge across the lake to the site, and horizontal reinforced concrete beams were placed on top of the pilings to form the superstructure of the fountain, 60 feet in diameter. Three miles of wiring controlled its lights; when the fountain debuted, the complete lighting sequence ran 18 minutes with a power output of 60,500 watts. "It's just what I dreamed it would be," the architect said.

But if Mr. Allen had been inspired by the picturesque fountains of Europe, some folks observed at the time, wouldn't you expect something more like those bubbling Roman wonders in *Three Coins in the Fountain* and other movies? Had anyone seen an electrified plastic bubble in Rome? For some, the Lake Eola fountain must have been a shock at the time, but now, years later, it has become the closest thing downtown Orlando has to an icon, its green plastic bubble a permanent part of the city's mental landscape, a survivor from the Fabulous Fifties that debuted under Sputnik's October skies.

Just a few days after Orlando turned on the fountain for the first time, the city was shocked by more serious front-page news: the crash of an Air Force plane that killed four, including the pilot, Colonel Mike McCoy. Visitors to Orlando in the years since may not have heard of the colonel, but anyone who has departed or arrived at Orlando International Airport has borne his stamp. The standard abbreviation for the big airport on tickets and luggage stickers is not OIA, as one might expect, but MCO, for Colonel Michael N.W. McCoy. After his death, Pinecastle Air Force Base was renamed McCoy Air Force Base in 1958. When the Air Force vacated the base in 1974, in became McCoy Jetport, Orlando's commercial airport, the precursor of OIA.

McCoy was commander of the 321st Bombardier Wing at the Pinecastle base and "a dominating figure in Orlando's civic life," the *Sentinel* said, when the B-47 Stratojet he was piloting passed over Orlando's College Park neighborhood and crashed near Ben White Raceway, now the site of the city's Trotters Park. The tragedy struck on October 9, McCoy's 52nd birthday. Three others were killed with McCoy: Group Captain John Woodroffe, 43, of the Royal Air Force; Lieutenant Colonel Charles Joyce, 38, director of operations of the 321st; and Major Vernon D. Stuff, 39, chief of the wing's bomb division.

By 1957, McCoy had logged more flying time than anyone in the Air Force: 20,000 hours in the air. He had set a B-47 speed record from London to the United States. "As he climbed aboard the plane on his last flight, Colonel McCoy lifted a clenched fist and yelled 'Charge,' as was his custom," a report in the *Sentinel* said. The plane took off from Pinecastle Air Force Base at 10:12 a.m. for a routine jaunt around the area. "The explosion that disintegrated the plane over the raceway, Highway 441 and Walter Rose's pasture came at 11:08," the paper said. The B-47's wreckage was strewn for a distance of nearly 3 miles, but only one house appeared to be damaged, and it was unoccupied. Not one person on the ground "was even scratched by the tremendous explosion," the paper reported.

If the skies above Florida brought serious worries and tragedies in the 1950s, on the ground Orlandoans had a whole new kind of music to take their minds off their troubles. Dig it or not, rock 'n' roll was here to stay. When its leading icon, Elvis Presley, shook up things at Orlando's Municipal Auditorium for two memorable visits, a local reporter knew how to make the most of it.

She was Jean Yothers, who in later years would shape Orange County's historical museum as its first curator. In the 1950s, Yothers wrote a snappy "On the Town" column in the *Sentinel*. Almost every day she'd be there next to the comics, a smart young woman (often holding a telephone in her signature photo) who had the scoop and told about it with style. For girls growing up in the Orlando in the 1950s, Yothers offered a glimmer of hope that, yes, life might offer something more fun to do than be Beaver Cleaver's mother.

Years later, Yothers's memories of Presley's Orlando appearances in 1955 and 1956 offer reminders that behind the cliches—the curled lip, sideburns, and thank-you-vrrry-much—was a real young man from Memphis, just a couple years out of high school, who caused shock waves in the 1950s. Central Florida was no exception. First, there were his clothes. In the August 9, 1956 *Sentinel*, Yothers described for readers the bright green sport coat, black trousers, and white shoes that adorned the hip-shaking sensation the press had christened "the Pelvis," a name he detested. To understand the effect of his dress, let alone his singing, consider the fashion tips inside the same paper, in the section then called the women's pages. "For more years than most of us can now remember, the words 'dinner hat' have been synonymous with beautiful little nothings for the top of the head," the syndicated writer began. Now, larger, smart black velvet hats were being seen in the chic restaurants in New York. It's a safe bet the ladies in velvet hats were not dining with husbands or sons in flashy green coats and white shoes; think instead of the look of the menswear in *Leave It to Beaver*. But youthful expression in dress was about to take off in colorful and rebellious directions, and Elvis, who had invented his own flamboyant style as a teenager, had more than a little to do with it.

More important, there was the music. "He looks just like a hound dog in heat and sounds like a sick cat," one disgruntled parent told Yothers, whose columns made clear she thought otherwise. Even in his first Orlando appearance the year before, when he was at the bottom of a billing headlined by the young "hillbilly" comedian Andy Griffith, Yothers knew she was witnessing something special. "Twenty-year-old recording artist Elvis Presley is the hottest thing to hit Orlando since the Avalon Hotel caught fire," she told readers on July 28, 1955. "Elvis has a unique singing and guitar-strumming style that's sending the teenage female set to swooning and screaming."

With Scotty Moore on guitar and Bill Black on bass, Presley in 1955 had followed a long lineup of Grand Ole Opry stars such as Ferlin Huskey and Marty Robbins, as well as Griffith, who had made a splash on television variety shows. Colonel Tom Parker, who began representing Presley only a few days before the Orlando tour stop, had organized the show, and he knew what he was doing in putting his new boy on last. When "Elvis, Scotty, and Bill" finished off the evening, Yothers said years later, "the crowd went absolutely wild. . . . You knew this was somebody we should recognize as an up and coming star." And by his second Orlando appearance, in 1956, that's indeed what Presley was. His legendary *Ed Sullivan Show* appearances were still in the future, beginning about a month after he played Orlando in August. But in the year since Yothers had first seen him, he had heated up TV screens on shows hosted by Milton Berle, Tommy Dorsey, and Steve Allen.

Now he was front-page stuff. "Wiggling Elvis to Play Orlando Twice Today," an August 8, 1956, headline proclaimed. With a photographer in tow, Yothers headed backstage after one of two packed performances at a sweltering Municipal Auditorium to interview the country's leading sensation. Her clearest impression after more than 40 years? "A real nice kid," one still near the beginning of his transformation from a music-crazy Memphis boy into a social phenomenon. But even in his first Orlando appearance, back in 1955, Yothers had picked up on worrisome undercurrents in the torrent of fame that lay ahead. She wrote in July 1955:

> Now it's none of my business, but I think Elvis is pushing himself too fast. He's wearing himself out giving the customers more than their money's worth. I just wanted to say to him, 'Slow down, boy . . . your fame won't disappear,' but he still goes like a house afire.

She was right on all counts. Decades later, Presley's fame is greater than ever, and audiences pay to see performers who train long and hard to sound as much like him as they can, to capture a flash of the feeling. But sadly the nice young man from 1955 and 1956 would be gone at 42, perhaps worn out from not slowing down, from simply trying to keep up with being Elvis.

ORLANDO

The summer after Presley's second visit to Orlando, another "king" landed in town and was hit by his own steamroller of fame. Writer Jack Kerouac arrived a published but struggling writer and left a best-selling author, crowned the king of the Beat generation. It was a title he didn't care for, although he surely was happy with the royalty checks and recognition that hit him headlong after his novel *On the Road* was published in the fall of 1957.

Kerouac's time in Orlando from July 1957 to April 1958 was "a critical period in his career," says Bob Kealing of The Kerouac Project of Orlando (Kerouac returned to live in Orlando again in the early 1960s). Not only did the writer rise to fame during his time in Orlando in the 1950s, but he also pounded out another novel, *The Dharma Bums*, in 11 days and nights in November and December 1957, streaming the words through a rented manual typewriter onto a 110-foot roll of teletype paper. Kealing, a veteran reporter for Orlando's WESH-Channel 2, has been on the trail of Kerouac's life in Florida in his spare-time research since a friend told him about the writer's Orlando connection in 1995. In 1997, Kealing co-founded The Kerouac Project with Marty Cummins of Chapters Cafe and Bookshop. With support from public and private donors, the nonprofit group was able to buy the College Park house where Jack lived and wrote. The project sponsors a writers-in-residence program that offers writers a chance to spend time in Kerouac's former digs, rent-free, to further their work.

A few miles from the College Park bungalow where Kerouac wrote *The Dharma Bums*, one of the Orlando area's best-loved spots for a Sunday stroll or drive in the late 1950s was Genius Drive in Winter Park. It's still there, though not open to the public. The "Genius" has nothing to do with a high I.Q., although the drive's owners did have plenty of smarts. Genius Drive takes its name from the family of Jeannette Morse Genius (1909–1989), Central Florida artist, interior designer, philanthropist, and visionary par excellence.

If anyone could be deemed Central Florida aristocracy, in the best sense of the word, it was Jeannette Genius. She founded and, with artist and educator husband Hugh McKean, built what would become the Morse Museum of American Art in Winter Park, along with the world's most comprehensive collection of the art of Louis Comfort Tiffany. In the 1950s, at a time when Tiffany's Art Nouveau–era treasures were out of favor with most art critics, Jeannette and Hugh McKean knew better. In 1957, they journeyed to Long Island, New York, and rescued many of the late art-glass master's signature works from the ashes of his mansion, Laurelton Hall.

Jeannette Genius McKean's grandfather was Charles Hosmer Morse, the wealthy Chicago industrialist who first visited Winter Park in 1881 and saw great promise in the town. In 1904, he became its biggest landowner and took over the Winter Park Land Company, of which his granddaughter would later be president. The year before Morse died in 1921, he acquired about 200 acres of oak-dotted land that bordered lakes Virginia, Mizell, and Berry. He planted orange trees and carved out an unpaved road, the start of Genius Drive. In 1938, with the aid of architect James Gamble Rogers, Morse family members built Wind Song, a Spanish-style mansion that would become the home of Jeannette and Hugh McKean in 1951, six years after their marriage in 1945. Soon they added the peacocks that would become the signature of the tree-canopied property, and a Central Florida institution was born.

Years later, after his wife's death and not long before his own in 1995, Hugh McKean would recall an exchange with a "pleasant young man" who had come to Wind Song to repair the telephone. "Do you live here?" the young man had asked McKean. "I grew up in Winter Park," the repairman continued. "I often walked through Genius Drive to see the peacocks. I always thought this place belonged to the city, or something like that." So did many other people.

Instead, the private road had long been opened without fuss as a gift of beauty to the public. As time went on, sad acts of vandalism forced the McKeans to close Genius Drive except for Sunday afternoons. In 1987, Hugh McKean told an interviewer that someone had shot one of the peacocks with an arrow. It had taken three days to find the wounded bird and care for it. Eventually, in the late 1990s, Genius Drive was closed to visitors all the time. In 1999, developers closed on the $35.5 million purchase of 160 acres of the original Morse holdings. The property, called the Preserve at Windsong, would be divided into 261 residential lots, the announcement in the *Sentinel* stated. The McKeans' house, Wind Song, would remain on a 40-acre tract set aside as a preserve, behind closed gates. The days when just-plain folks strolled or drove on Genius Drive on Sundays to see the peacocks were only a memory.

Near Wind Song and the museum Hugh and Jeannette McKean founded, hotelier Robert Langford brought big-city hotel style from Chicago to Winter Park in 1956, anticipating the Orlando area's future as an innkeeper to the world. Later lauded as a visionary about the growth of tourism, Langford was told he was crazy by some area pundits when he started planning a year-round Winter Park resort hotel in the early 1950s. At the time, most inns in Central Florida closed in summer. But Langford had a definite feeling about the future of Central Florida. In his view, air conditioning was key to the whole thing.

The Langford Hotel opened in 1956 with 82 rooms. An early guest was Roy Disney, Walt's brother and guiding light in business matters. "He asked me how many rooms I had," Langford recalled years later, "and when I told him 82, he said 'You'd better double it.' " Eventually, sections were added to the original hotel, and Langford's hotel grew to 218 rooms, surrounded in bamboo, bright-colored crotons, and other tropical flora. Under Langford's ownership, the hotel was long a favorite of European visitors. Especially in the pool area, it looked like Florida should; it even had its own flock of pink flamingos in the 1960s.

Langford's hotel and his flamingos had to weather a whopping breeze in 1960, when one of Orlando's most memorable hurricanes, Donna, blew through Central Florida. In 1960, hurricanes were decidedly female, and Donna was no lady. According to records compiled by hurricane experts, Andrew in 1992 tops the list in destruction of property (although not loss of life), with an estimated cost of destruction that approached $30 billion. The runner-up in destruction is Donna, with more than $300 million in estimated damage, according to research by Jay Barnes, author of *Florida's Hurricane History*.

Hurricanes started receiving names in 1950. The first ones didn't have the women's names so long linked to the storms. Number one was "Easy" in September 1950, followed by "King" in October. Donna, the destructive champ until Andrew came along, hit Orange County hard. Although the storm was a killer in the Caribbean and South Florida with 124 deaths to its credit, Central Floridians had days to prepare, and only a few minor injuries were reported. But flooding and wind-wrecked trees caused power outages that lasted for days.

"The electricity went off in the middle of the Miss America pageant telecast, and stayed off for five days," an *Orlando Sentinel* reader, Mary Ann Campbell, recalled in a 1978 story about the storm. Central Floridians were watching not only Miss America but also the 1960 Olympics and reports on the Kennedy-Nixon presidential campaign. The night before the storm hit, *Orlando Evening Star* television commentator Bill Summers noted that "CBS concentrated on women gymnasts." "The Russians had a couple of lulus—or is that luluvitches?" Summers quipped in the spirit of Cold War rivalry.

Late on Saturday, September 10, Donna knocked out power, making the tube a "useless piece of furniture," Summers wrote on September 12. In the days after "Dreadful Donna" swept through Orange County, according to the *Star*, Sam Roper of Roper's Grill at the Gateway Corner in Winter Park tried to cut loose the shredded remains of his $4,000 canvas awning. Before the storm, Roper had been trying to take it down when "winds knocked the ladder from under" him, and he wisely must have decided his life was worth more than the awning. He left Donna to rip it up royally.

A couple of years after the storm played havoc with Floridians' attempts to watch the Kennedy-Nixon debates on TV in 1960, the Kennedy presidency was in full sway in 1962 when the big Jordan Marsh department store arrived in Orlando with Camelot-era style.

JM provided the five-story finishing touch to the Colonial Plaza Shopping Center, which had opened its first section in January 1956. Colonial Plaza's initial row of stores paralleled Colonial Drive, which is also State Road 50, a major thoroughfare that cuts directly across the state from coast to coast. In the center's original procession of stores, Belk's was at the east end (separate from the main phalanx of stores), and Walgreen's was at the west. In October 1962, Jordan Marsh capped off a fresh addition to what was now a T-shaped shopping complex. If you think of the original strip of stores as the top of the T, the addition was its central pillar, 57 shops capped at the end by the behemoth department store with its name displayed in elegant script.

Colonial Plaza had become Colonial Plaza Mall, Central Florida's first, and Jordan Marsh was its anchor. At the opening, people packed the store to ride the escalator between the four floors of the store that displayed merchandise. (The fifth floor tower housed display storage and a work area.) So novel a feature was the four-floor automatic conveyance that uniformed representatives of Eastern Airlines were on hand on opening day to give "wings" pins to young riders who made the trip between floors. At the time, Eastern was the only major airline to serve Orlando's Herndon Airport, just to the east of Colonial Plaza.

If Robert Langford had brought big-city hotel savvy to Orlando, Jordan Marsh brought a new retail sophistication. It had real Christmas windows, with mechanized figures like you might see in Macy's or Bloomingdale's in New York. And it sparkled inside for the holidays, with themed decorations and displays of conversation pieces, such as a huge stuffed Steiff dinosaur or mink-trimmed lingerie. But here's the almost astounding difference between those days and now—the one that makes you want to weep if you remember the last time you traipsed in a mall store from cash register to cash register, practically begging someone to wait on you.

"We always had enough sales people to handle the customers," retired JM executive Larry Signorile remembers. It meant a staff of 30 in the toy department alone during the holiday shopping season, and 26 people in housewares. To a regular sales staff of hundreds throughout the store, managers added about 250 extra workers for the Thanksgiving-to-Christmas buying blitz. Like the regular sales people, they went to training classes. They learned not only how to work a cash register but also how to greet customers graciously. No one was better at greeting than the store's dapper manager, Henri Guertin, always attired in an immaculate suit and tie. During the holidays, Signorile recalls, Guertin got a kick out of pulling a red wagon around the store to help customers with their packages.

It was a symbol of the many services Jordan Marsh offered. You could have gift purchases shipped directly from the store, and there was no charge for home delivery on the store's own trucks. As many as 17 tailors stood ready to make your newly purchased garments fit just right. And if you were feeling peckish or wanted to meet friends, you might head to the elegant Oakmont restaurant on the fourth floor, where shoppers could relax with a meal or a martini, if the spirit moved them.

And the day before Christmas? "It was panics-ville," Signorile says. That was "the day husbands walked though the stores bleary-eyed," practically bumping into things in their search for the perfect present. Hectic? Yes. Stressful? Maybe. But here's the reason, perhaps, the ghost of the big store beckons still, especially on Christmas Eve. Like a lot of the late 1950s and early 1960s in Orlando, as Signorile says, "it was a lot of fun."

Chapter Ten

A WHOLE NEW WORLD

In 1962, American business pundit W.M. Kiplinger was keen on Florida. The state had the makings "of a great new empire, now only in its beginnings," he wrote in the preface to a book titled *Florida: Land of Fortune*. There was money to be made, plenty of it, especially in tourism, the state's leading industry. But too much puffery circulated about the Sunshine State, Kiplinger said. Investors needed hard-headed business information, and he wanted to give it to them.

The book grouped Orlando—Florida's biggest inland city, with a population of 88,000 in 1960—with Gainesville, Ocala, and other low-profile spots in Central Florida, an area of the state with the "sort of serenity that captivates" tourists, Kiplinger said. "One of the major tourist delights of the winter season" in Orlando was to sit and listen to band concerts at Lake Eola, Kiplinger cohort Stephen Flynn wrote in *Florida: Land of Fortune*. Flynn dubbed the area's many lakes the biggest local tourist attraction. If visitors wanted to see something special, they could drive a few miles up U.S. Highway 17, just south of Sanford, to take their picture by the Senator, 47 feet thick and billed as the largest cypress tree in the nation.

What these pundits could not have known was that only a couple of years later, a man who first made his mark as an artist, not a business leader, would change the face of Central Florida forever, making the name "Orlando" recognizable to most people from Tokyo to Tel Aviv. After Walt Disney's dreams materialized, in 1971, Orlando would face a whole new world.

In 1964, Disney was scouting inland Florida to find a site for an East Coast version of his Disneyland theme park, located in Southern California. Flying over vast expanses of undeveloped Central Florida land, he spotted the place 15 miles south of Orlando where the Florida Turnpike crossed construction for what eventually would become Interstate 4. Disney had wanted the new attraction on a piece of land so big that it couldn't be surrounded by the competitive clutter he disliked around Disneyland in Anaheim, California.

Although he didn't quite get as good a price as the Dutch who bought Manhattan from the local inhabitants 300 years before for $24, he pulled off in secret one of the most spectacular land deals of all time. In the end, Disney's company paid a little more than $5 million for 27,443 acres, about 43 square miles, or twice the size of Manhattan Island.

Opening in October 1971, Walt Disney World began with the Magic Kingdom. Epcot, MGM Studios, Animal Kingdom, water parks, hotels, night clubs, and restaurants followed. By the 1980s, the Disney complex would become the world's largest tourist attraction. By the mid-1990s, more than a billion people would pass through its gates. By 2000, Disney World's more than 55,000 workers made it the nation's largest single-site employer and the backbone of the Central Florida economy. Competitors, Universal Studios and SeaWorld to cite just two, would follow and expand also. By 1998, those working directly in the tourism industry made up 14 percent of the total local workforce, and almost half as many again were indirect results of tourism.

"More people have experienced the Pirates of the Caribbean than live in the United States today," wrote the authors of *The New History of Florida* in the mid-1990s. And Orlando, the pleasant, small city with the band concerts in Lake Eola Park, had become the tourist capital of the world.

The man who made it happen remains, as Richard Schickel wrote in his book *The Disney Version*, "one of the most significant shaping forces in American culture," a man whose "ever-lengthening shadow continues to shade it in curious and intriguing ways."

According to most accounts, Disney's boyhood was not easy. When he was nine, in 1910, he got out of bed each day at 3:30 a.m. with his older brother Roy to help their father deliver newspapers in Kansas City. He told an interviewer years later:

> The papers had to be stuck behind the storm doors. You couldn't just toss them on the porch. And in the winters there'd be as much as 3 feet of snow. I was a little guy, and I'd be up to my nose in snow. I still have nightmares about it.

But the early hours weren't all the stuff of bad dreams. He recalled:

> On nice mornings I used to come to houses with those big old porches, and the kids would have left some of their toys out. I would find them and play with them on the porch at 4 in the morning when it was just barely getting light. Then I'd have to tear back to the route again.

The other boys who worked for Walt's father, Elias Disney, to deliver 3,000 *Kansas City Star* newspapers each morning in 1910 were paid $3 a week. Walt and Roy Disney, eight years older than his little brother, were paid nothing.

Few Central Floridians know it, but the Disney family had ties to the area long before Walt changed the face of the state. Walt's parents had married in a Central Florida ceremony in Lake County on January 1, 1888, about 45 miles north of Orlando. The county had formed on May 27, 1887 and issued its first marriage license exactly seven months later for the Disney-Call union. Their famous son missed being a native Floridian by just a few years.

The late *Orlando Sentinel* journalist Ormund Powers sketched out the story a few years ago, quoting from a history of the Paisley, Florida area in Lake County. Walt Disney's maternal grandparents were Charles and Henrietta Call, who were living in Greenfield Township, Huron County, Ohio, in the 1860s. The Calls moved to Ellis, Kansas, in 1879 and after five years resettled to what is now Lake County to escape the harsh winters. Their Kansas neighbors, Kepple Disney and his son, Elias, also came to Florida. The Disneys settled near what is today Paisley, and the Calls acquired 80 acres about a mile north of the settlement (then in Orange County), Powers wrote. The Call children were Flora Call (Walt Disney's mother); Jessie Call, who married Albert Perkins in 1887; Grace Lila Call, who married William Frary in 1890; Julia Call, who married Lawrence Campbell in 1897; and Charles Call Jr.

Kepple Disney returned to Kansas in 1887, but Elias, Walt's father, stayed behind and, on January 1, 1888, married the eldest Call daughter, Flora, in the little Kismet church. She was almost 20; Elias was almost 29. The couple soon moved to Daytona Beach, and their oldest son, Herbert, was born in Florida in December 1888. Later they moved to Chicago, where Elias worked as a carpenter. A second son, Raymond, was born there in 1890, followed by Roy in 1893, and Walter Elias Disney in 1901. The boys' lone sister, Ruth, joined them in 1902.

In 1906, the family moved to a 48-acre farm near Marceline, Missouri, on the mainline of the Atchison, Topeka and Santa Fe Railroad, about 100 miles northeast of Kansas City, the city to which they migrated a few years later during the paper-route era.

Back in Florida, Walt Disney's uncle Albert Perkins, who had married Walt's mother's sister Jessie Call, became the postmaster of Paisley in 1902 and served until 1935. Jessie Call Perkins taught in several Lake County schools and eventually served as principal of Eustis High School. When her husband died, she succeeded him as postmaster and served until 1946. The story goes that the young Walt and Roy Disney visited Jessie and Albert in Florida during their summer vacations from school. "Grace Parker Guenther, one of the authors of a history of Paisley, believes that Walt's familiarity with Central Florida was why he chose to place Walt Disney World here," Powers wrote.

If the young Walt Disney did enjoy vacation time in Florida, it must have been one of the bright lights in a boyhood shaped by hard work and his father's harsh discipline. It's likely he did find enjoyment in drawing, even at an early age. One story has it that his first brushwork used tar, which sat in a barrel on the farm to be used for patching roofs and fixing drains. "When he was 6 or 7, Disney seized the brush, dipped it into the barrel and proceeded to decorate the white walls of the farmhouse with large and fanciful drawings of animals," the story goes, as it is repeated in Schickel's book.

The boy kept on drawing, encouraged by a gift of paper and pencils from an aunt and by a local doctor's kindness. He really did enroll in those correspondence-school cartooning courses—the kind you used to see advertised on matchbook covers—and when he was 14, he joined a Saturday morning art class at Kansas City Art Institute. That was 1915, and he was just a boy. But perhaps in some small way, Walt Disney had found a niche to lodge his dreams. Schickel writes:

> A childhood grounding on hard economic bedrock can be invaluable to a man who spends his adult life in a highly speculative enterprise like show business with its sudden, often shocking, ups and downs. It teaches one how much worse things can be.

Another man who helped change Central Florida not long after Walt Disney World opened in 1971 was much less well known than Disney, but a pioneering spirit nevertheless. In 1973, on January 15, 58-year-old Arthur "Pappy" Kennedy took the oath of office as Orlando's first black city council member, the city's first black elected official, period. "I'm happy to be here," he said, "and I'm ready to go to work."

It had been a hard road for Kennedy. For years black people in Orange County had not had much greater success in trying to vote than July Perry and Mose Norman had back in 1920, when the Ocoee Riot was sparked by their attempts to partake in the democratic process. In the 1940s, black people in Orange County were effectively disenfranchised by a Democratic

Party committee called the White Voters Executive Committee. (The Democratic Party in the South in the first half of the twentieth century was a far different institution than it is today.)

At a time when Florida was a one-party state, not being able to vote in the Democratic primary meant not being able to vote at all, for all practical purposes. That changed after four black Orlando residents challenged the committee's control in court, and in October 1950 Orlando had the first primary, at least since Reconstruction times, open to men and women of all races.

It would be more than 20 years, though, for a black person to gain a seat on Orlando's governing board. Council elections then were at large, which meant a candidate had to draw votes from the whole electorate instead of his or her district. When Kennedy first tried for the council seat for District 4 in 1967, he already had a long record of public service. Eve Bacon's history of Orlando describes his efforts in 1946, as the executive secretary of the Negro Chamber of Commerce, to boost a community-wide project to send food to starving war victims in Europe.

Kennedy lost his first try for office in 1967, but he came back in 1972. In a race with echoes of the 2000 electoral drama in Florida, he narrowly won the machine-count of ballots but gained the council seat only after a four-month court battle over contested absentee ballots. (In this case, the absentee votes were ultimately thrown out.) Four years later, in 1976, Kennedy won a second term resoundingly.

Almost everyone, it seems, called Arthur Kennedy "Pappy." The story goes that his grandmother gave him the nickname as a small child because he walked like an old man. Whatever the origin, it was an endearment often given to gentlemen of Kennedy's generation who commanded affection and respect. Pappy Kennedy drew plenty of both.

The youngest of three children whose parents were killed in an auto accident when he was three years old, Kennedy was first reared by his grandmother in the Panhandle community of River Junction. He moved to Orlando when he was about 12 to live with his aunt and uncle after his grandmother died. Kennedy graduated from Jones High School during the early 1930s, when as a teenager he also began working as a bellman at the old Orange Court Hotel, which stood on North Orange Avenue across from the *Orlando Sentinel*'s present-day location.

As years passed, Kennedy became a waiter, eventually at Winter Park's popular Barbizon restaurant on Park Avenue. The eatery transformed into the Beef and Bottle restaurant, where he was assistant manager at the time of his 1972 victory.

When he declared his intention to run, Pappy Kennedy made a statement that still sounds remarkably fresh years later: "As Orlando continues to grow into what will inevitably be a large metropolitan area with a great influx of people of great diversity, it is time that all segments of the population be given true representation and an opportunity to participate" in governing their city and determining their future.

The future: Both Disney and Kennedy heard its call. Two men from such far different worlds, they might not appear to have much in common. But both had come from hardship; both had worked and dreamed their way to lives far different than their beginnings might have predicted. Like the pioneers who had carved a place for later generations on the palmetto prairie long before, and like so many who had touched the beautiful city's past, they knew the power of dreams.

SELECTED BIBLIOGRAPHY

Argrett, Leroy, Jr. *A History of the Black Community of Orlando, Florida*. Fort Bragg, CA: Cypress House Press, 1991.

Bacon, Eve. *Orlando: A Centennial History*. 2 vols. Chuluota, FL: Mickler House, 1975.

Barber, Mary Ida Bass. *Florida's Frontier: The Way Hit Wuz*. Gainesville, GA: Magnolia Press, 1991.

Beatty, Robert L. II. "Legacy to the People: Community and the Orange County Regional History Center." Master's thesis, University of Central Florida, 2002.

Birkhead, Patricia J. *We've a Story to Tell: A History of the First Baptist Church, Orlando, Florida, 1871–1996*. Franklin, TN: Providence House, 1996.

Blackman, William Fremont. *History of Orange County, Florida, Narrative and Biographical*. Deland, FL: E.O. Painter Printing Co., 1927.

Bordelon, Pamela, ed. *Go Gator and Muddy the Water: Writings by Zora Neale Hurston from the Federal Writers' Project*. New York: W.W. Norton & Company, 1999.

Boyd, Valerie. *Wrapped in Rainbows: The Life of Zora Neale Hurston*. New York: Scribner, 2003.

Brotemarkle, Benjamin D. *Beyond the Theme Parks: Exploring Central Florida*. Gainesville, FL: University Press of Florida, 1999.

Cole, Julie, Wilbur Allaback, and Laura Stewart. *Orlando's Leu House*. Orlando: Harry P. Leu Gardens, 1995.

Covington, James W. *The Billy Bowlegs War*. Chuluota, FL: Mickler House, 1982.

———. *The Seminoles of Florida*. Gainesville, FL: University Press of Florida, 1993.

Crow, Myrtle Hilliard. *Old Tales and Trails of Florida*. St. Petersburg, FL: Osceola County Historical Society and Byron Kennedy and Company, 1987.

Dann, Carl. *Carl Dann's Vicissitudes and Casathropics*. Orlando: Florida Press, Inc., 1929.

Deagan, Kathleen and Darcie MacMahon. *Fort Mose: Colonial America's Black Fortress of Freedom*. Gainesville, FL: University Press of Florida and Florida Museum of Natural History, 1995.

Edwards, Wynette. *Orlando and Orange County*. Charleston, SC. Arcadia Publishing, 2001.

Florida: A Guide to the Southernmost State (Federal Writers' Project Guide). New York: Oxford University Press, 1939.

Fries, Kena. *Orlando: In the Long, Long Ago, and Now*. Orlando: Kena Fries, 1938.

Gannon, Michael, ed. *The New History of Florida*. Gainesville, FL: University Press of Florida, 1996.

———. *Florida: A Short History*. Rev. ed. Gainesville, FL: University Press of Florida, 2003.

Gore, E.H. *History of Orlando*. Orlando: Academy Press, 1949.

Guide to Florida's Historic Architecture. Gainesville, FL: University Press of Florida, 1989.

Hann, John H. *A History of the Timucua Indians and Missions*. Gainesville, FL: University Press of Florida, 1996.

Jahoda, Gloria. *Florida: A History*. New York: W.W. Norton & Company, for the American

Selected Bibliography

Association for State and Local History, Nashville, TN, 1976.

Kaplan, Carla, ed. *Zora Neale Hurston: A Life in Letters*. New York: Doubleday, 2002.

Kealing, Bob. *Kerouac in Florida: Where the Road Ends*. Orlando: Arbiter Press, 2004.

Mahon, John K. *History of the Second Seminole War, 1835–1842*. Rev. ed. Gainesville, FL, | University Press of Florida, 1985.

———. *Florida's Indians from Ancient Times to the Present*. Gainesville, FL: University Press of Florida, 1998.

———. *The Timucua*. Cambridge, MA: Blackwell Publishers, 1996.

Miller, Clyde R., ed. *Miller's Orlando City Directory, February 1907*. Reprinted. Orlando: Central Florida Genealogical Society, 2002.

Moore, Joyce Elson. *Haunt Hunter's Guide to Florida*. Sarasota, FL: Pineapple Press, 1998.

Moore-Willson, Minnie. *The Seminoles of Florida*. Philadelphia: American Printing House, 1896.

O'Sullivan, Maurice and Jack C. Lane, eds. *The Florida Reader: Visions of Paradise from 1530 to the Present*. Sarasota, FL: Pineapple Press, 1991.

Powers, Ormund. *Martin Andersen: Editor, Publisher, Galley Boy*. Chicago: Contemporary Books, 1996.

Rajtar, Steve. *Orlando Greenwood Cemetery Historical Trail: A Visit with Over 425 Historic Orlandoans at Their Final Resting Place*. Orlando: Central Florida Genealogical Society, 2003.

Read, Robert W., ed. *Nehrling's Early Florida Gardens*. Gainesville, FL: University Press of Florida, 2001.

Robison, Jim and Mark Andrews. *Flashbacks: The Story of Central Florida's Past*. Orlando: Orange County Historical Society and the *Orlando Sentinel*, 1995.

Robison, Jim. *Kissimmee: Gateway to the Kissimmee River Valley*. Charleston, SC: Arcadia Publishing, 2003.

Rogers, William Warren and James M. Denham. *Florida Sheriffs: A History, 1821–1945*. Tallahassee, FL: Sentry Press, 2001.

Ste.Claire, Dana. *Cracker: The Cracker Culture in Florida History*. Daytona Beach, FL: The Museum of Arts and Sciences, 1998.

———. *True Natives: The Prehistory of Volusia County*. Daytona Beach, FL: The Museum of Arts and Sciences, 1992.

Schickel, Richard. *The Disney Version: The Life, Times, Art and Commerce of Walt Disney*. 3rd ed. Chicago: Ivan R. Dee, Incorporated, 1997.

Shofner, Jerrell H. *Orlando: The City Beautiful*. Tulsa, OK: Continental Heritage Press, 1984.

Swanson, Henry F. *Countdown for Agriculture in Orange County, Florida*. Orlando: Henry F. Swanson, 1975.

Thompson, Geraldine Fortenberry. *Orlando, Florida*. Charleston, SC: Arcadia Publishing, 2003.

Tinsley, Jim Bob. *Florida Cow Hunter: The Life and Times of Bone Mizell*. Orlando: University of Central Florida Press, 1990.

Tucker, Cynthia Grant. *Prophetic Sisterhood: Liberal Women Ministers of the Frontier, 1880–1930*. Boston: Beacon Press, 1990.

Weisman, Brent Richards. *Unconquered People: Florida's Seminole and Miccosukee Indians*. Gainesville, FL: University Press of Florida, 1999.

Winter Garden Heritage Foundation. *All Aboard! A Journey Through Historic Winter Garden, 1880–1950*. Winter Garden, FL: The Foundation, 1997.

INDEX

Index

ORLANDO